UNDER THE APPLE TREE

One Season's Reflections

UNDER THE APPLE TREE

One Season's Reflections

JENNIFER WIXSON

Copyright © 2018 by Jennifer Wixson
All rights reserved.

Paperback ISBN 978-0-9962237-8-2
eBook ISBN 978-0-9962237-5-1

No part of this book may be reproduced or transmitted in any form or by any means, electronic or mechanical, including photocopying, recording, or by any information storage or retrieval system—except by a reviewer who may quote brief passages in a review to be printed in a magazine, newspaper or blog—without permission in writing from:

White Wave Publishing
P.O. Box 4
Troy, ME 04987
whitewavepublishing@gmail.com

This book is lovingly dedicated to my late mother
Rowena Mae Palmer,
1932-2017.

AUTHOR'S NOTE

This little book is comprised of excerpts from the nature journal I kept the summer after my mother's death. Sitting out under the apple tree scribbling in my journal—refreshed by the sights, sounds, and scents of the natural world—I found peace and healing after our unexpected loss. Death is never a welcome visitor, but I discovered that Mother Nature and her friendly ambassadors provide a good antidote for those of us who are left behind.

Did someone say that there would be an end,
An end, Oh, an end, to love and mourning?
Such voices speak when sleep and waking blend,
The cold bleak voices of the early morning
When all the birds are dumb in dark November—
Remember and forget, forget, remember.

After the false night, warm true voices, wake!
Voice of the dead that touches the cold living,
Through the pale sunlight once more gravely speak.
Tell me again, while the last leaves are falling:
"Dear child, what has been once so interwoven
Cannot be raveled, nor the gift ungiven."

~ from "All Souls" by May Sarton

TABLE OF CONTENTS

PHOTOGRAPHS

Rowena Mae Palmer

Some of our Scottish Highland cows enjoying the delights of the pond

My neighbor's lilacs

Mother Bluebird

My wild bee nest box on the fencepost

Mr. Chippy

My close-up pic of Walter the gray tree frog

Miracle swarm of honeybees on the way to my empty hive

Some of our cows and calves relaxing in the field next to the pond

Mom's amaryllis bloom in Mr. Chippy's water dish

Cranberry Man on the ATV

My wild bee nest box, with some of the tubes filled

Hay waiting to be tedded

The pond as seen through the trees

My honeycomb, packaged for sale

My gladiolas and sour cherry pie

Postcard to my mother from May Sarton, atop Sarton's 1966 book of poetry

Me shelling peas on our front porch

The four quarts of blackberries I picked the other day

Cranberry Man working at our project house, putting up his homemade clapboards

Mom's grave in Norway Pine Grove Cemetery

My lawn chair under the apple tree next to the herb garden, with the fence and my John Deere tractor in the background

An apple on my special tree

Delilah's calf, separated from its mother (again)

May 24, 2017

Under the Apple Tree

Anger has driven me to pick up a pen and begin this new journal, I admit to myself, as I idly watch a small sweat bee going about her business pollinating the apple blossoms that drape like a pink-and-white parasol above my head. I write sitting under the old apple tree out behind our house, the sweet scent of apple blossoms wafting down to me on the light breeze. The breeze quivers the green tassels of a nearby pine and inspires the small hands of an oak tree down by the pond to wave at me, catching my attention. How much easier it is to live with trees than with people!

A loud "snap" like the breaking of a water-sodden branch interrupts my solitude, if one can call this solitude inundated by the whirring and chirping of tree frogs; the calls of crows; the buzzing of wild bees in the blossoms overhead; the music of a mysterious warbler; the wind rustling the trees; and the faint droning of traffic out on Route 9. There! The snapping sound again, as though some Thing looming large is slogging thru the deep wet woods on the opposite side of the pond. Our Scottish Highland cattle are entertaining themselves today in the pasture near my husband's woodshop, which means the foreign noise I am hearing, and it is progressing—snap, thud, pause, snap—is not a bovine.

Since the natural world is going about its business regardless of the noise (the gray tree frogs now sound like chimps in the trees fighting over a banana) I'm inclined to think the sound is nothing to fear. Most likely the creature disturbing my solitude is a moose, wandering around gamely and gauntly looking for fresh green shoots. We do get lone males that amble thru our rural corner of central Maine every few years, awkward-looking beasts, but no uglier than our hairy, long-horned cows, I suppose. The presence of moose rankles my husband, who must fix our electric fences after the moose passes thru. Deer will lightly jump the electric fences, buff-colored ballerinas that they are, leaving nary a trace of their visit, except perhaps a parting of the meadow grass where they have lightly touched down. By contrast, moose are insensitive creatures, inured to electrical jolts. They are plodders rather than jumpers, sometimes dragging strands of fence wire into the woods with them for hundreds of feet.

Well, the black flies have found me. That did not take long. I have barely settled myself into my chair under the apple tree for a heart-to-heart chat with this new journal when a cloud of black flies floats in and lands on me like soot. Only the females bite and suck blood, so rather than begin swatting and instantly doing battle with the bugs, which only calls in *more* black flies, I wait to see whether I have hungry ones or just visitors. Today the black flies appear to be just visitors. And now the breeze has picked up, lifting the insects and pushing them en mass like a black cloud toward the raspberries. One of the reasons I selected this spot for my repose is just because of this faithful breeze, my old friend. The breeze generally blows up from the northwest, picking up steam in the meadow behind me and whisking across the water and up the hill to where I sit. This refreshing northwest breeze typically carries with it the fresh scent of the woods from the far side, the dank and mysterious smell of the pond water, and whatever floral scent Mother Nature has chosen to arrange, which today is the sweet perfume of old-fashioned apple blossoms from this one surviving apple tree by the frog pond on my husband's family farm. The old apple provides a delightful place to seek solitude in the cool shade on hot summer days when there is no place else to hide from the heat and humidity, from endless labor, and from unwanted visitors.

I should say something about the pond, lest anyone envision something as grand as Walden Pond. First, there is no inlet to the pond. Instead, fresh water comes from rain, run-off from the rain, and from one mysterious spring hidden deep within the pond's black depths. Second, there is no outlet. Water evaporates or dribbles out one corner during heavy rains or is imbibed by our cows. The result of the first and second facts is that there is no regular coming and going of fresh water thus no coming or going of fish. Having no fish in the pond explains a good part what resides in this ecosystem, which is mostly frogs, turtles, and toads. A pair of mallards that stopped at the pond this spring stayed less than an hour, which was long enough to convince the mating pair that one of our back ponds was more conducive to raising young than this one. The mallards would rather share the smaller but deeper back pond with a gaggle of Canada geese than run the risk of their cute little ducklings becoming turtle food, consumed by one of the humungous snapping turtles, which like the smaller but more populous painted turtles consider this particular pond as the perfect tenement for their type, thanks to the presence of partially-submerged logs, tree limbs, and stumps that give the turtles plenty of places to sun themselves and yet still be able to plop into the water like flat rocks—the tossing kind—whenever I venture too close.

Ah! I had to finish writing that last long bit and so I did not get to the black fly in time and she has chewed deep enough to draw blood. I squash her and the blood smears down my arm, drying quickly in the light breeze.

I have a warbler here beside the pond, too. I'm not very good at identifying bird calls, despite years of half-hearted study, and so I've been unable to identify what I think is some type of warbler, always very careful to hide himself away up high in the leafy screen provided by the trees that line the pond: pine, maple, poplar, black locust, and birch. For the past two or three years when I have sat here, I have nearly driven myself half-mad trying to identify this regular summer resident that loudly serenades me with birdsong—the same four notes repeated with varying inflections—what seems like 24-7. Finally, I just decided to relax and enjoy the serenade rather than ruin my precious time under the apple tree by attempting to categorize something that has no knowledge that it is being categorized, pinned down, described, named, recorded, and discussed in detail by birders.

Now, a chickadee sends out a call, which sounds like that of the phoebe only without the garble in the back of the throat that is so distinctive of the flycatcher. The warbler had momentarily taken a breather, relinquishing the floor, and so the chickadee whistled "phee-be, phee-be" to fill the void and immediately attracted a reply, from whom, I do not know. Hopefully, a potential mate.

I opened my mouth (after putting the pen down) to take in a gulp of water and in flew a black fly. Naturally, I sucked her way into the back of my throat. Instinctively I swallowed. There! One less black fly to worry about.

The mosquitoes have found me here under the apple tree, too. Not many, just one or two whining about my lawn chair attempting to reconnoiter the situation before calling in all their relatives. Either my blood or my blood type has not met their standards for after one or two attempts to latch on the mosquitos have absconded.

The snapping noise in the woods has stopped, but now is replaced by the *putt-putt-putt* of my husband on his ATV, no doubt checking fences around the pond. This pond, my favorite, fronts up against Route 9, although it is rarely glimpsed by motorists speeding past. I had to confess to my husband recently that whilst mowing the small strip of grass that separates the pond from the road (and leads to the mother-in-law's abode) that I accidentally smacked into one of the cedar fence posts with the riding lawn mower while ogling several turtles sunning themselves. I cracked the old gray fence post nearly in half. Now, I did not have to confess my fender-bender; I could have held my tongue and let my husband (around here we call him the "Cranberry Man" and I might as well introduce him as such at the start of this journal) assume that the cedar post had succumbed to age and moisture or even to the heavy snow load we had last winter. But sometimes (actually, most of the time, if I'm honest about it, which I really think is a good part of my problem) I can't seem to help myself—I tell the truth, which often is not a good thing for the truth-teller. I've discovered the hard way, which is the way I learn best, apparently, that truth invites anger, criticism, condemnation, hurt feelings, and a whole lot of angst and stress to be heaped upon me, which is often why I seek peace here by the pond under the old apple tree. (Perhaps I should substitute "leisure" for "peace" in that last sentence since the tree frogs sound like they are fighting over the bananas again.)

Today the apple tree is showering me with her fragrant and rejuvenating blessings. White silken petals slip off the blossoms and mingle in the air with tiny tufts of dandelion seed. The petals and fuzzy tufts waltz around each other like miniature ghosts, dancing and turning in the few gleams of sunlight that make their way thru the leaves of the gray branches.

In fact, it was just such anger and angst heaped upon me—a sibling's anger and angst relating to our mother's passing—that caused me to take up my pen and pillows and begin this new journal. Only now that I have been scribbling under the apple tree for nearly an hour, I find that my own anger has cooled and my hurt dissipated. I hope my sibling finds similar solace soon.

Some of our Scottish Highland cows enjoying
the delights of the pond.

May 26, 2017

Lilacs

How quickly the lilacs die!

A few hours ago, I pilfered an extravagant number of lavender lilac bunches, dew still dripping from their florets, from my neighbor's bush (my neighbor no longer having use of them in this mortal world) and stuck them into a great jug of water in the house. The lilacs immediately filled our little home with their fragrance. I thrust my nose into the center of the bunch, inhaling deeply their healing scent.

When I was a young girl—maybe eight or nine—my grandmother took me with her to prepare the family cemeteries for Memorial Day. We cut copious lilac blooms from her ancient bushes and arranged the blossoms in metal, forest-green cemetery vases that we stuck into the ground in front of the graves of our Dearly Departed, some of whom I noticed had been departed an awfully long time. How lush and gorgeous those lilac sprays looked highlighted against the old gray slate and white marble tombstones! How shocked I was when I returned with my grandmother two days later to collect the containers and unceremoniously dump the limp, wilted lilacs into the woods on the other side of the black iron fence! I had expected to have my delight repeated on that second visit and was cruelly awakened to the realities of death and dying—and I did not like it. Nor do I like death and dying to this day.

My neighbor's lilacs.

June 2, 2017

Mother Bluebird

A gusty wind is blowing today. The gusts turn the white-lined page before I have finished scribbling on it, and blows my long hair into my eyes so I can hardly see to write. It's a chilly northwesterly wind and I notice that dark thunder clouds have moved in, piling on top of one another. The barometric pressure is obviously falling. The chickadees are squeaking out peculiarly high notes, as though being squeezed by an unseen hand. Two sparrows—who were lovey-dovey only a few minutes ago—are now fighting in the nearby oak. For once, the tree frogs are silent, gone to ground for the duration of the storm, possibly afraid of being struck by lightning if they remain in the tall trees.

I consider my options. Stay where I am under the apple tree and get wet *or* pack up shop before I have said what I want to say.

One gust of wind comes at me like an emotional outburst. It gets tangled up in a nest of oak leaves, which rustle magnificently, magnifying the sound, making the wind seem much worse than it is. I elect to stay and take my chances. The storm will likely blow over and leave me dry, albeit with plenty of dust and tree pollen in my hair.

The delicate red and white blossoms of my new perennial bleeding-heart bob up and down in the breeze. The yard exhales the scent of freshly-cut grass and moist, mulched leaves from last fall that nature tucked for safe-keeping into depressions in my herb garden and raspberry patch. I am happy to be journaling again, relieved to have the luxury of time to converse with myself, to find out where I am in life now and where I (possibly) am going. Of course, I have learned the hard way that we never do truly know where we are going until we get there, and often we learn long after we have arrived.

The sky is weeping now. Nothing major, just a few fat drops to splotch the blue ink of my ballpoint pen and wet the pillow holding the journal in my lap, as though I have cried myself to sleep on it.

I learned the hard way this spring with the unexpected death of our mother, who certainly wasn't supposed to die yet. I certainly thought my mother was "safe," at least until my father passed away. Even my father expected Mom to outlive him, I think, because he is one year older and, well, because that's what men do; die first.

But Mother experienced a classic female heart attack. Because the symptoms didn't present as a typical (male) heart attack, Mom thought she was having indigestion. She powered thru the next week, despite a major valve blockage—singing in the church choir, volunteering at the library, visiting friends in the nursing home—until her heart had nothing left but to blow itself up. A week after her original heart attack, Mom allowed she "probably ought to go to the hospital."

By then it was too late, although we didn't know that. A surgeon at Maine General tried to save her, but unfortunately Dr. Hero only prolonged her life, precipitating an extra two months of pain and suffering for Mom. Eventually, however, we were able to spring Mother free from the hospital and remove her to her home where she experienced a grace-filled, peaceful death with all her family around her.

The flutter of the female bluebird's wings awakens me from my scribbling, which is headed toward an emotional diatribe. Ah, yes! Here I am, under the apple tree. Mother Bluebird, another old friend along with the NW breeze, reminds me that life is for the living, and not for the dead.

Mother Bluebird has been setting on eggs in the bluebird box that Cranberry Man affixed to the cedar post at the end of our row of old-fashioned blackberries. The berries are a terribly thorny variety, but the sweetest-tasting blackberries in the world. This is the third year in a row Mother Bluebird has been with us. For many years all we had in the box was barn swallows. But then I thought to remove the old swallow's nest four years ago, and ever since we have had Mother Bluebird here rather than a swallow.

One would never know Mother Bluebird is in the nest box most of the time. In fact, I mowed around the blackberries earlier today, studiously avoiding meeting her eyes every time my head went round and round barely a foot from the entrance hole. I discovered the first year with Mother Bluebird that if I am so presumptuous as to look directly at her, she will fly out of the box, almost smacking me in the face. Now, however, we have come to an understanding. Mother Bluebird hunkers down on her eggs whilst I mow, only the top of her head and beak visible as I slowly mow the blackberries near the box. (I do occasionally sneak a peek.) I always give her a heads-up when I'm drawing nigh, although obviously Mother Bluebird hears the hum of the riding lawn mower approaching. I never start with the blackberries, but save them for last, working my way toward them as though perhaps I'm not actually going to mow them this time. Later, after I've finished mowing and returned the mower to the barn, I come on foot to watch from a respectful distance as Mother Bluebird feasts on the bugs the lawnmower has liberated. She pops out of her pine bluebird box when the mowing is done and lands on a low-hanging limb in the nearby peach tree. From there, she surveys with apparent glee all the insects upon which she can gorge. Her outing is short-lived, however, as there are always those eggs to keep warm. Someday soon, however, she will have chicks to feed and plenty of bugs to feed them.

I'm grateful to Mother Bluebird for awakening me from what could have been an extended bout of self-pity today. Grief is fine, but self-pity is not good for the soul and never returns one's investment in it.

The solitude I find under the apple tree is a balm to my senses. Every flutter of a bird's wing, every flashing shimmer of sunlight on the surface of the pond, every cool breath of air on my cheek is precious. I drink the precious dram deep, feeling my heart expand with contentment.

I have decided that there will be two rules for this journal. (One must have rules to give a piece of writing form and structure.) The first rule is that I never read what I have previously written before taking up the pen to add a new entry. This allows the writing to progress naturally, with thoughts and feelings unfolding organically rather than being driven by intellectual purpose, rationale, or something like self-pity. And the second rule is that I write only under the apple tree so that my words are directed as much by Mother Nature as by me. She, one of God's busiest evangelists, is the rock upon which I have built this journal.

The rain comes down in earnest now. I can no longer remain in denial—I must go inside.

Mother Bluebird.

June 4, 2017

Wild Bee Nest Box

A wild bee has discovered the wild bee nest box I hung up on the fence post near the apple tree a couple of weeks ago. As I set my pillows and journal into the lawn chair, I heard a little buzzing noise near my right ear. I glanced up just in time to see some wild bee zip away from the wooden nest box. I leaned closer to inspect the tiny round hollow tubes stacked upon one another like cordwood in this outhouse-looking little box and, sure enough, the end of one of the hollow tubes—the third one up from the right—was packed with fresh mud.

I purchased the natural pollinator nest box—an Apoidea they call it (which is actually the superfamily name for bees and wasps)—as a lark, not expecting such a silly thing to be utilized by our native bees, which after all, have plenty of places to nest on our 150-acre farm. So, I am surprised and delighted to discover that my $10 purchase might become more than an interesting conversation piece.

I've now turned my chair around from my usual venue so that I can keep an eye on the nest box as I write. I'm curious to know which of our wild bees has succumbed to the lure of this store-bought bee condominium and how she goes about her business. As a beekeeper, I'm ashamed to admit how shockingly ignorant I am about native pollinators, although we did put in a 1/8th-acre planting of a New England wildflower mix as part of our farm grant from the NRCS two years ago. The planting is now heavily populated with goldenrod, bee balm, anise hyssop, lupines, and various grasses and weeds. The butterflies seem to like the wildflower mix (which my husband swears is nothing more than "damn weeds"); however, I've only ever seen a couple of large carpenter bees creeping out from their hidey-holes in the low-growing grass.

Now the chipmunk—who I recognize as Mr. Chippy, an acquaintance from last summer—has chosen to move to a tree nearer to me and "cheep" away at me like a broken record. I guess I have invaded his personal space. I should have known, as I know from last season that Mr. Chippy has a nest under the wooden pallet on which my forlorn-looking, empty beehive sets, about eight feet away from my chair.

My honeybees died over the winter (as they did the previous winter) and I can no longer afford the $140-$150 per five-frame nucleus of bees that beekeepers are charging these days. Instead, I'm keeping the drawn comb and some honey in the empty hive in the crazy hope that a swarm will take up residence. Catching a swarm depends upon having a poor beekeeper in the area, one who fails to split a strong hive and thus the bees split themselves, with half seeking a new abode. It is early days yet to collect a swarm, however. The best time for swarming is when the black locust trees come into bloom. I don't know if there are any other beekeepers near me. The only beekeeper I was aware of, the octogenarian gentleman across the road, called it quits beekeeping two years ago. Perhaps—like me—he has been unable to resist the siren song of the honeybees? But with his decades of experience, he would be unlikely to lose a swarm.

Mr. Chippy reminds me with his constant scolding that I was descanting about him. He has a winter home under the pallet on which the hive rests. (The pallet itself sets upon stacks of black slate about a foot-high.) I know this interesting fact about Mr. Chippy because I've seen him tank up on sunflower seeds at my many bird feeders, and then scoot away with his loot in a circuitous route for the pallet. So, my proximity to his winter feeding ground is causing Mr. Chippy understandable frustration. Perhaps he thinks (if chipmunks think, that is) that I will move the pallet and retrieve my stolen sunflower seeds.

The air is damp but fresh today, having been washed by a few passing showers. We are still in that discouraging late spring weather pattern where one minute it is sunny and 70° and the next it is rainy and 50°. It has been so cold at night (often below 45°) that the wood frogs and gray tree frogs haven't been mating. The spring peepers still perform their duties, however, and sing out their sonorous song in the evening, sounding like sleigh bells in the distance. Cranberry Man has hardly worn his earplugs at night this spring. I'm not sure what CM was thinking when he built this new house in the meadow between a frog pond and a vernal pool, but the result is that we have a delightful racket (in my opinion) here in the evenings and at night from about mid-April thru mid-August. Visitors to the farm are always amazed by how loud the tree frogs in particular are and even I was, too, when I first arrived on the scene nearly ten years ago.

Since I turned my chair around, I have seen no activity in the wild bee nest box. I wonder if the wild bee came and laid her eggs and then closed them off from the world with mud until it's time for them to hatch. Will she return to dig the mud out and release them like my honeybees chew the caps off the new bees in the brood cells when the newbies are grown enough to join the swarm? If so, she (the wild bee) must also deposit enough nourishment for her young to consume during this time. And how many eggs does she lay per hollow? Will she return to lay more in another hollow tube? Seems like a lot of work—laying the eggs, providing them sustenance, and then packing mud in the end of the tube—for one small bee to do. How much time and effort it must take!

For the first time this season I hear the "rhuum" of a bullfrog in the pond. In a few weeks, their rather distinctive mating calls will add a nice bass to the chorus of the spring peepers and the chirping and purring of the gray tree frogs. The wood frogs, with their garbled, duck-like chuckles, have been notably absent this year (except for a few nights in early spring). I'm worried about the poor things, wondering if last year's drought has negatively affected the wood frog population.

From this vantage point—viewing Life in the opposite direction than usual here under the apple tree—I am gazing upgrade at my sweet little herb garden. The woodruff is still in bloom, small white blossoms scattered like late-season snow in amongst the taller herbs. The bee balm, Lady's Mantle, blue globe thistle, Valerian root, rhubarb, and bunching onions are going gang-busters. The sage and thyme are lagging, but I know these favorites for drying and fresh cooking will catch up and surpass the early-birds, which plants will flare out mid-July and certainly by August. I remove my right sneaker and toss it into the middle of the herb garden. The tennis shoe bounces off a big bunch of creeping thyme, releasing a burst of dry, sweet scent like that of eucalyptus. I lean back in my chair, close my eyes and inhale deeply. The fresh thyme scent relaxes me. I love to sit near the herb garden just for this reason—it's my personal aromatherapy patch, which together with my apitherapy patch (the bee hive and now the wild bee nest box) treat most of the malaise of the human condition. The balance of my stress is generally taken care of by the soothing purr of the tree frogs.

But I would really like to know more about natural pollinators, especially Maine's native bees. I've had such difficulty lately (as have thousands of beekeepers around the country) keeping my honeybees alive. Who is to say whether it is colony collapse disorder (CCD) or the neonicotinoid insecticides utilized in the growing of genetically modified corn that is killing them? Unfortunately, one of our farmer friends grows GMO corn in fields on either side of us. I thought about educating him on the negative effects of neonicotinoids on honeybees, but decided, cowardly, to let sleeping dogs lie. I never had trouble keeping bees twenty years ago. In fact, I met the Cranberry Man on the one-acre bog of Stevens cranberries he planted in 1998. I stopped by to see if he wanted to rent a hive or two of my honeybees to pollinate his cranberries. At the time, I managed fourteen hives. Despite knowing that the natural pollinators did the trick perfectly fine for the cranberries, CM invited me to bring my bees over. Thirteen years later, we were married. But if the honeybees are dying off—and the natural pollinators are disappearing as well—what are we farmers to do?

Wait! Activity at the wild bee nest box. A small, very small, sweat bee has arrived. She bounces in the air in front of the box a few times as though deciding which hollow tube to select. Then she quickly alights in one of the top tubes and crawls inside. I keep count of the seconds. At twenty-five seconds she comes out, crawls into another hollow hole, and repeats the process. This the wild bee does several times. I do believe she is laying eggs in each round tube. I don't think this is the same bee I saw when I first arrived, since she is not a buzzing bee and is certainly smaller.

Well, this show is quite intoxicating! I have already received $10 in enjoyment and in educational value watching this bee. I am very curious about the mudding part, though. When will that commence? Will this small sweat bee mud off the ends of her tubes like the bigger, buzzing bee did? Or will she just lay her eggs and depart? How long will it take her eggs to hatch? Is it twenty-one days to hatching like it is for worker honeybees (and chickens)? Truly, watching the activity at the wild bee nest box is as fascinating as watching my honeybees come and go from their hive, as I usually do when I sit here. Perhaps it is even more fascinating because there is so much I don't know about the natural pollinators.

Mr. Chippy takes his protesting diatribe to a new level and a new tree. You would think by now after several years of using the apple tree as my occasional al fresco porch he would realize I'm likely to be here at least an hour (two or three if I can stretch it) and that I am inured to his constant complaining. Last year, by late June, Mr. Chippy would leave off protesting (proselytizing?) after half an hour and then run right past me in the lawn chair en route to his treasure under the pallet. I hope he gets used to me quicker this year!

The sweat bee has returned (she flew off a paragraph or two ago and I forgot to mention it as so much else was going on). I wonder, is she laying eggs or bringing in mud now? When I leave, I'll peek inside.

Mr. Chippy suddenly quits squeaking. Two tree frogs immediately fill the void, trilling out love notes from alternate trees. The mysterious warbler in the treetop begins his melodic chirping again. The bullfrog "rhuums." The sweat bee returns and keeps working away at the nest box. The wind rustles thru my herbs, releasing their sweet scent. I do believe we have reached that magical interlude in the afternoon when it is time for me to set my journal down on the ground, pull up the chair's footrest, close my eyes, and daydream.

Later that afternoon

I checked the wild bee nest box and Mrs. Sweat Bee did not mud off her tube ends, at least not yet. And the end of the original mudded-off tube has dried to a light-brown color, matching perfectly the color of the tube itself. If I hadn't appeared on the scene just as my mysterious wild bee (who has not returned) was finishing up her work, I would never have suspected that her eggs were inside. I can barely wait the three weeks to see if the eggs will hatch and what my new arrivals will be. I make a mental note to mark my gardening calendar, where I keep track of such things, when I go inside. There is always so much to look forward to on the farm in summertime! Things growing, hatching, mating.

Oh, dear! Now there is a pathetic crying coming from a maple tree over near our hay barn, where the swallows nest. I suspect some predatory bird has eaten or stolen a barn swallow's eggs. Poor thing! I can't help but empathize with her. All that work! And perhaps close to fruition, too. Does the barn swallow think that her cries will help bring her eggs back again? Or is her audio outpouring a natural expression of bird grief?

I know that animals have feelings, certainly our Scottish Highland cattle do. These cows are some of the smartest and most feeling animals I have ever known (and I have known a lot, having been born on a dairy farm, worked for a large animal vet while in high school and upon graduation went to work on a dairy farm in Woodsville, N.H.). I've watched our cows experience a wide-range of emotions, from envy to fear to jubilation to the fondness of love and friendship. But I've never thought much about the emotional life of birds (sounds like a good book title) partly because they always seem so cheerful.

The poor mother swallow has now given up her wailing and fluttered off. Will she abandon her nest altogether because it has been despoiled? If so, will she set up housekeeping someplace else? Will she lay more eggs to replace these?

I could google the answers to my many nature questions—so many questions arise each afternoon in which I take my repose under the apple tree! But it is far more interesting, rewarding, and *real* to learn from Mother Nature herself.

The tree frogs are purring in earnest now. Late afternoon is melting into early evening. In the distance I hear a jet flying overhead, coming from or going to Bangor International Airport. The clouds have gathered overhead, dimming the light and making the many colors of green jump out and reveal themselves. The rest of the world seems so far away from me here under the apple tree, as though I'm living on a magical moon, one that revolves around Earth but never connects. I wonder if this is how the birds and the frogs and the bees view me, as one whose world revolves around theirs but never connects with it. Perhaps they don't even "see" me at all. No, that is not the case. Thank God for Mr. Chippy—angry verbose Mr. Chippy! For he at least lets me know my presence has been noted, even though I am obviously downright annoying to this Nervous Nellie. One likes to be noted, after all.

Mother Nature surely has a sense of humor, for no sooner did I declare that I wanted to be noted—to feel as though I was a "seen" member of the natural world—then she answered my prayer by sending in a whining mosquito. The pest landed on my neck and inserted her stinger as expertly as a phlebotomist. I whacked the mosquito and the fresh blood proceeded to draw in hordes of her relatives, a not-so-subtle reminder to be careful what you wish for.

I hop up out of the lawn chair and retrieve my one sneaker from the herb garden, gather up the pillows, and make a run for the house. There is such a thing as being too popular with the locals!

My wild bee nest box on the fencepost.

June 7, 2017

Mr. Chippy

The sun is finally shining today after a series of gloomy, cold, and wet days. I worked on my new novel this morning, which is late in production because I was unable to write this winter and early spring while helping care for my mother. After Mom's death I was unable to pick up a pen for more than a month because I was so weighted down with grief. I felt anchors on my soul. I have righted the ship, however, and returned to my writing, my second vocation, after farming.

My mysterious unknown warbler lets out a series of melodic chirps not far from where I sit. He is down low to the ground, an unusual thing for this bird. Perhaps today I will catch a glimpse of my songster?

The breeze is from the south; the wind carrying the warm weather up the eastern seaboard. Today it is 75°. Tomorrow we might hit 80°. That won't be soon enough for my aching bones!

Mr. Chippy rustles in the dead leaves on the other side of the electric fence. The fence around this pasture, which includes the piece of woods behind me, is only inches from the back of my chair. Mr. Chippy exits the pile of leaves, spies me in my usual spot, and then skips on past me with nary a scold. It is magical! He has come to accept me already this summer. I wonder if he remembers me from year's past? Do chipmunks have memories? Lucky for them if they do not.

The grass is still wet, but—warming from the sun—the ground releases a delicious fragrance so strong I can taste it. I do not need to brush up against my herbs to catch a whiff of the bee balm and horsemint today, either. The air is rich with the fragrance of herbs.

My chair is turned around from its usual vantage point, so once again I am facing uphill on this slight incline, which is rather awkward when I put the chairback down as the blood rushes to my head. But being backwards I can keep an eye on my wild bee nest box. I came prepared today with a penlight and a magnifying glass. When I first arrived under the apple tree this afternoon, I inspected the Apoidea. While examining the insides of the tiny hollow tubes in the nest box, I felt much like my dentist must feel examining my mouth. Curiosity has been my constant companion since I can remember. When we were growing up, our mother encouraged us kids to follow where our curiosity led us. Unfortunately, over the years my curiosity has landed me in some awkward places. So far, I have managed to survive, however.

Out of the corner of my eye I see Mr. Chippy creeping up the fence line toward me. Oh, lord! It is too funny. He has obviously been visiting my bird feeder because his cheeks are puffed out two inches on each side. Mr. Chippy seems to be searching for a suitable location to hide this particular loot because as he creeps, he stops, and then starts up again. Now he is standing up, sniffing the air. Now, crouching down and sniffing under the leaves at a stray sunflower that (surprise!) has taken root in the rich soil under the fence. This is what happens when you drop a seed or forget where you bury it, Mr. Chippy! It grows.

Mr. Chippy suddenly stands up on two legs, as though about to give a circus performance. To my surprise, he tilts up a large dead oak leaf, taller than himself (how did he do that?) and proceeds to stuff the rounded tip of the leaf into his already full mouth. Then he disappears under the leaf, pulling the brown blanket over him in a vanishing trick worthy of Barnham and Bailey. (Sadly, I recently heard that B&B has closed up their tents for good after nearly 100 years.)

There has been no activity at the wild bee nest box since I've been writing. Two of the empty hollow tubes are no longer empty since my last visit to the apple tree, however. These two tubes have a soft white filmy substance stopping their ends, which looks rather like a cocoon. When I arrived, I examined them closely with the magnifying glass and penlight. One "cocoon" was opaque, but the other had 2-3 very tiny holes chewed thru as though the creature inside was chewing its way out. I experienced an uncanny and slightly creepy sensation that I was being observed even as I was observing. I snapped off my penlight and stepped quickly away. How would I feel if someone or some Thing unexpectedly turned a spotlight and magnifying glass upon me in my house?

As I scribble in this notebook, I watch for Mr. Chippy to reappear. I'd like to know the secret to his vanishing trick. Don't we all want to know how the magician performs his tricks? And yet aren't we disappointed and feel let down when we do learn the secret? Indeed, maybe I really don't want to know all of Mother Nature's secrets.

After lunch, before retiring to the apple tree for my day's reward, I replanted my peas and beans—for the second time. The spring was so cold and miserable that very little grew at first planting. I did get germination on my beets, spinach, Swiss chard, and carrots, but those were planted only last week. I also planted my basil and pepper seedlings this afternoon, taking a chance that we will not get a late season frost, which is probably a mistake because the full moon is coming up soon. "Why run the risk?" I ask myself. Nevertheless, I could not stop myself from putting the seedlings in the ground, it was such a fine day.

A barn swallow lets out a loud few "cheeps" as she flutters past my chair. I think that is the swallow's alarm call for when predators get too close to her nest. She lands on one of my nearby raspberry canes (my rows of raspberries and blackberries are only 10-15 feet away) and bobs up and down. I keep an eye on her and perhaps vice versa. I wonder if she has a nest near me? Was she the poor swallow whose nest was despoiled recently? As I watch, the swallow spies a bug in the grass, swoops down, and snatches the creature up. She flies away. I hope she is going back to her nest to feed her young.

The leaves are rustling again, this time from about 20 feet away. I swivel quickly toward the pond and spy Mr. Chippy leaping from a downed branch to dead log. He stops suddenly when he reaches a large, moss-covered rock, only a small part of which sticks out of the ground. I glance away. When my eyes return to the rock he has disappeared. No, wait! There he is again, weaving over the ground and getting closer and closer. I think Mr. Chippy knows I'm watching him and is now taking the roundabout route back to my bevy of bird feeders. I have five bird feeders altogether on the back lawn, not far from our kitchen and dining room windows.

At 4 p.m. I am meeting my Unity College volunteer Samantha at Scoops Ice Cream in Unity. Today is Sam's birthday. She's 21, that special age where one can legally drink alcohol. Since I no longer imbibe (30 years next year – August 5, 2018) I substituted another sinful substance with which to celebrate her special birthday—ice cream. Samantha will be a junior at Unity College in 2018-19 and has helped us here on the farm, especially with our two acres of cranberries—hand-weeding, harvesting, cleaning, sorting, bagging—since the summer before her freshman year. She took a summer class on food production and I hosted one of the classes that year. Although we had 25-30 students here that day, Samantha alone stood out. She helped me serve refreshments after my al fresco lecture and then helped me clean up. When Sam volunteered to help us with the cranberries it was a no-brainer. Since that day we have come to be extremely fond of Samantha and consider her to be part of our little family here in Troy.

Well, I have completely lost sight of Mr. Chippy now, but I'm joined by the female woodpecker, who I suspect has a nest in the large maple tree, which stretches proudly upward and outward and looks like Jack Spratt's wife compared to this spindly apple tree. Now I hear soft squawking and short cries emanating from the mysterious green mass of leaves above me. The woodpecker must be feeding her young. Or perhaps she is talking to her eggs like our Scottish Highland cows talk to their unborn babies? Our cows moo softly to their unborn calves so that after the babies are born, they recognize her voice and can discern which animal is their mother.

Mr. Chippy has begun to squeak, that monotonous, one-note barrage. And now Cranberry Man has started the riding lawn mower and is headed this way. I see I will have no more rest and repose under the apple tree this afternoon.

Mr. Chippy.

June 8, 2017

Walter the Gray Tree Frog

Today is one of those glorious summer days in Maine that you dream of in the doldrums of winter: 84° with a dry NW breeze, just enough to keep the bugs at bay and to offset the heat. The solar panels we installed earlier this month (after many years of saving and planning) are cranking out electricity. Our Maine-made Pika inverter feeds the power to the house first and then the extra electricity goes to the electrical grid. I love the idea of being a power generator rather than a consumer. By noon we had generated 23kw, not very much in the grand scheme of things. But every grand scheme, like every great tapestry, starts with a single thread. I like being one of those threads.

The breeze is very fresh-smelling, coming as it is down from Canada, rushing over the pond and up the hill to where I sit here under the apple tree. I have my chair turned back to my usual vantage point so my head is now uphill and legs downhill, and I'm looking away from my Apoidea and gazing down the short stretch of mixed hardwoods to the pond. Yesterday I noticed that the pond water was covered with green pine pollen. Today the pollen is all blown to the eastern side of the pond, leaving the dark surface clear enough to ripple with the wind, wrinkling the mirror image of the trees lining the opposite shore.

Grass is growing up in the shallow areas of the pond, areas laid low by last year's drought. My chair overlooks mostly the shallow end. With its pollen, islands of grass, and water-logged dead tree limbs, the pond from this angle would not be considered attractive to anyone, except moose, turtles, and frogs.

Speaking of frogs, I'm afraid I might have given a mature tree frog a heart attack yesterday afternoon. After folding up my chair and returning it to the hay barn, I came back to collect my pillows and journal, when I was jumped by the sudden loud chirping noise of a gray tree frog. Another tree frog faintly responded, a female I assume, and soon the two began a series of courting trills. The loudest wooing song emanated from a maple tree at the end of an old wood pile near the barn. I've been a frog lover since childhood; therefore, the notion that I might discover the hiding place of a tree frog was irresistible. Earlier in the year while surfing the web I found the herpetologist's website, herpmapper.org, and ever since then I've been longing to post a frog sighting from our farm. In fact, in early spring I even ventured out into the vernal pool near our house attempting to catch mating wood frogs. I was unsuccessful in all but getting my tall barn boots filled with water. The boots weighted me down so much I was nearly forced to abandon them in the muck; however, I finally pulled myself and my boots out of the mud, wet to the waist.

The loud trilling of my excited tree frog emanated from a distance easily within my camera's reach. The frog seemed to be about three or four feet up the tree. I approached the maple cautiously and quietly, but he must have heard me or felt the vibration of my footfalls because the critter immediately fell silent. (Frogs are awful "shaap.") As a result, I couldn't pinpoint his exact location on the tree. Still, I examined the trunk, which was about four-feet around, my heart pounding. I was keenly aware that Maine's gray tree frogs (*hyla versicolor*) can change color from light green to gray-brown to a mottled, spotted combination of the colors, thus blending in perfectly with the gray bark. I ran my hand over the rough tree trunk, patting it down like a policeman pats down a suspect. Nothing! Very frustrating. I stepped back to consider the maple from another angle and noticed what I hadn't seen earlier—a large, flat-faced, healed section of the trunk that was obviously where a low branch had split or broken off years ago. The scar had naturally stretched as the tree grew. From several feet back, the scar appeared sunken into the trunk and perfectly healed. But upon closer inspection I found a cavity or pouch behind the top section of the scar, about the size of a small change purse. Sure enough, tucked down into the bottom of this pouch was a very large tree frog. I was so excited I whipped out my phone and snapped several pics, which turned out terrible. All I got was the black interior of the mysterious hollow. Determined to nab a photo for herpmapper.org, I turned on the flash and stuck the camera over the top of the hole, flashing away. The phone covered the hidey-hole like a roof, so the frog couldn't escape. I ended up with several close-up photos of the gray tree frog, looking chagrined and disgruntled, his cheeks expanded like balloons at a kid's birthday party. I did feel a bit bad about disturbing him, especially when the poor fellow failed to return to his mating song after I left him alone. In fact, he fell silent completely.

I checked on the tree frog several times last evening, but he never sang again. The bright lights of the flash must have been too much for him or perhaps his ego deflated (along with his sacs) after our encounter. Today I have not dared to peer into his hidey-hole, thinking that at least I would give him another day to recover or to vacate the premises before my curiosity intrudes again.

There is sort of a nutty scent in the air today, as though what smelled moist and dank yesterday dried out overnight. The nutty scent is overlaid with a sweetness, which source I've had difficulty pinning down. The bridal wreath in front of the house is in full bloom and exudes a sweetness almost akin to that of strawberries, which makes my mouth water in anticipation of what Cranberry Man has said will be a banner crop of that rich red fruit in 3-4 weeks. My periwinkle-blue delphinium is in bloom about 20 feet away, but the breeze is blowing its scent in the opposite direction.

Nevertheless, I can't stop myself from rising and going over to sniff the blue delphinium blooms (nada) and on my return to the chair, I notice my spot is about three feet away from the sweet woodruff still in blossom. Of course, I would have noticed this had my chair been turned round the other way, but I find I cannot look forward and backwards at the same time. This occurs when reviewing one's life, too—we have difficulty considering the future when mired in the past. I generally prefer to sit in my chair so I can gaze out over the pond, because this is Maine and one of the unwritten laws (and there are many) is that one must rusticate or repose near water in summer. The pond, unprepossessing as it is, is my best possibility.

As I sit and write two maple seeds helicopter down and land on the pillow in my lap. The small one in unremarkable, a rust color like that of dried pine needles and about the length of my thumbnail. The larger seed, however, is a glorious mauve, as though the seed was blushing for its part in the reproductive operation of the maple tree. Finely-etched veins sweep up the flat wing from the swollen seed head, giving it the appearance of a fairy's wing broken off from her back. Surely, she must be nearby looking for her lost wing?

An eastern-tailed blue butterfly flutters past on a circuitous route somewhere. Overhead, a chipmunk, not Mr. Chippy, chatters away in an annoying fashion. I am getting used to blocking out this creature's incessant scolding, having discovered by listening to him thru an open window in the kitchen earlier that I am not the offending party, responsible for the racket. My good friend Mr. Chippy, who these days scurries past me in the chair with reckless abandon, has not presented himself yet, though I have heard occasional rustling and hopping sounds in the dead leaves in the woods, so I think he's nearby. Perhaps the other chipmunk is trying to move in on Mr. Chippy's territory?

I have nicknamed my photographed frog, whose existence I recorded on herpmapper.org (my first!)—thus putting our farm on the map—Walter. I don't know exactly why I selected that name, except that his expression of disgust reminded me of a Walter I once knew. That other Walter, a former boyfriend, frequently appeared to disapprove of my actions and life choices. I am dying to know whether I have killed Walter (the frog Walter, of course—I know the human Walter is still alive). I am exercising my powers of control, which is not my greatest strength, to stop myself from leaping up and checking out Walter's hidey-hole. But I have mentally promised poor Walter a reprieve from me until tomorrow, and so, Walter, if you do have hyper-sensitivity that enables you to know what I'm about to do, you are forewarned.

White, fluffy clouds gather from the south. We had hoped to make even more solar power today than we did yesterday—46kw—the day being a few minutes longer, but I'm afraid Mother Nature has other ideas. Whenever I find myself making assumptions about the natural world, I soon discover I'm almost always wrong. This would be discouraging if Life wasn't so darn interesting!

Now that I've had my fun, it's time to go to work. My novel needs attention. I completed two chapters in the last two days, which was wonderful, except that I wrote so fast I'm ahead of my storyline and I'm not sure where to "go" next. I need to take some time and think—just think—about the plot. I need to be present with my characters. To do that I must put down my pen, close my eyes, and just be. Fortunately, it is such a perfect day, and I'm in a perfect spot, for being!

My close-up pic of Walter the gray tree frog.

June 11, 2017

The Tent Caterpillar Nest

Oh, what a blessing it is to retire under the apple tree and relax for an hour or so! Currently, the thermometer (which is in the sun) registers 92°. It is at least ten degrees cooler here in the shade, with the most delightfully moist breeze blowing up from the pond.

Two or three tree frogs begin chirping. The breeze smells like pond water today. Puzzle pieces of sunlight pass thru the rustling branches overhead and fall on the pillow in my lap. The pieces of light shift about like the moving light reflected from a faraway mirror.

Before I could take to my chair, I had to destroy a forest tent caterpillar nest that recently appeared in the apple branch above me, partly responsible for my shade (the apple branch, not the caterpillar nest). Cranberry Man alerted me to the presence of the nasty, white tent. "Didn't you notice it?" he asked. "It's right over your head!"

Well, no, I had not noticed. Me, who is sitting here writing a nature journal! I guess there are just so many other things that have highjacked my attention: the native bees, Walter the tree frog, my herbs, the various scents carried upon the breeze, etc. etc. I never got around to looking—up! I destroyed the nest just in time. The caterpillars had matured and were in fact already on the move, pulling their blue-striped bodies up the slender apple branch to look for a good "V" neck in which to set up shop. I snatched up the white webbing with my bare hand, pulling it away from the branch like a bunch of cotton candy, taking care to position a hot, soapy pail of water beneath the nest. The smart caterpillars drop to the ground when you touch them, where they can live to crawl back up the tree and build their nasty nests another day. But I am smarter and catch the drops even as I thrust the web-full of squirming caterpillars into the killing water. I splash some hot, soapy water on the branches, washing away their little dark feces. Then I feel each slender branch and twig in the fork carefully to ensure I have captured and killed every caterpillar.

I have always hated tent caterpillars, despite my fondness for all things natural, because once they leave the nest the mature caterpillars start chomping on fresh green leaves and defoliate my trees. The creepy creatures seem to want to start with my favorite trees, too, as though deliberately denuding what I love best: my little plum trees, the ornamental crab CM planted the first year he built this house, the pair of matched sour cherry trees I planted when I joined him here and which cherries make absolutely the best sour cherry pie, and every apple tree on this property.

I must change the killing water two or three times because it quickly becomes black with the bugs, their feces, and what remains of their tents after I've torn them from the trees with my bare hands. From May 1st on, I repeat this death march once a week, at least into mid-June, until I can find no more tents to take down. I've discovered that by beginning my Pest Management Plan early in spring, I can reach my victims from the ground. It's only the second and third generations of tent caterpillars who manage to make their way up to the unreachable tops of the tall trees, where one typically spies a superabundance of white, tent-like nests in defoliated trees late summer and early fall.

My mother-in-law was taught to destroy tent caterpillars by cutting off the host branches and burning them and the tent. But this is overkill, both for the bugs and for the host tree. As long as you're not afraid of getting your hands dirty the hot, soapy water trick works just as well. Also, this method leaves the trees intact.

I pause to kick a spider off my right foot. Now I see, by looking closer, the offending bug is not a spider, but an ant. Several more ants are climbing up the arm of my chair. I don't really like ants, either. I was forced to move my chair up near the herb garden today to find the shade. Apparently, I have situated myself upon an ant's nest.

Quickly I hop up, brush off the ants, and yank the chair down the hill eight or ten feet, close to the electric fence line, yet still in the shade. I've never won a battle with ants (unlike with the tent caterpillars) and now I no longer try—I simply retreat. My personal belief is that ants will eventually take over the world. Someday there will be nothing left but ants and cyborgs with artificial intelligence, and these two will duke it out. My money is on the ants.

An acquaintance saw my post on Facebook about my homemade remedy to rid your trees of tent caterpillars and sent me a link about the benefits these pests provide. Fortunately, I couldn't open the link and so I did not run the risk of having my opinion about these nasty creatures altered.

I'm happy to report that I did not kill poor Walter the tree frog. I checked his hidey-hole (finally) and discovered it was vacated. So, Walter is still alive somewhere. What a nice, dry spot his hidey-hole is! Almost like a miniature kangaroo pouch. No wonder Walter selected such a comfortable, dimly-lit spot to try and woo his girlfriend(s) to!

A tree frog now trills romantically from the rugged trunk of a maple tree about 15 feet away. I imagine that it is Walter, serenading me. Ah, it is such a joy-filled song! "Walter, Walter—sing a song for me." He begins to purr like a contented cat, happy no doubt to see me.

No wonder I didn't discover the tent caterpillar nest above my head all these weeks. I spend so much of my time here in delusion!

June 19, 2017

The Miracle Swarm of Honeybees

A miracle has happened! A swarm of honeybees has taken up residence in my empty beehive.

Last Wednesday, late in the afternoon, I was chatting with Cranberry Man in our kitchen, my back to the sink, when suddenly he interrupted the conversation with: "Look! A swarm of bees."

I turned around and spied thru the kitchen window what looked like a very low, golden cloud. Sunlight was reflecting from the gossamer wings of an airborne swarm of honeybees! The swarm moved like an other-worldly cirrocumulus cloud. "They're going into the hive," I cried ecstatically. "You don't know that," CM dismissed me. "I do. Watch!" Sure enough, within five minutes the swarm completely disappeared, as though sucked up by my waiting and welcoming hive. My beehive must have seemed like Paradise to these honeybees on a search for a new home. The warm and dry hive comes with a good roof and is complete with drawn brood comb, honey, and pollen—everything honeybees need to thrive. No wonder the scouts found it!

Today the bees are working the black locust blossoms hard. I wrote back on June 4th that the most likely time to catch a swarm is when the black locust blooms. Well, how right was I?

Their first day in the hive the honeybees spent completely cleaning house. They dragged out all the dead, dried bodies and body parts of their predecessors and tossed them over the edge of the landing board. After house cleaning, the bees commenced bringing in nectar and putting up honey. They are working the snow-white blackberry blossoms in addition to the ivory-colored, drooping blooms of the black locust trees. On the fourth afternoon I smelled fresh honey being dehydrated. The rich, sweet scent wafted out from the hive. Smelling the honey, I suspected it was time to add the supers (extra boxes for the excess). When bees swarm, they engorge on honey before they exit their old home, carrying with them these old stores into their new house. To hold that old honey, the "new" honey already in the beehive, and the honey they are now bringing in they will need more room (in addition to the brood comb in the two boxes). It's always best to check first before adding supers, however.

So, I suited up. After smoking the bees and removing the outer and inner covers, I spied the tell-tale bright white new honeycomb fleshed out between the tops of the wooden frames, signaling that indeed the frames were full of honey. I added two supers, one of which was a set-up for Ross rounds. A super of Ross rounds (named for its inventor) can produce thirty-two half-pound units of honey in the comb, which when removed from the super snap into round plastic cassettes. Our farm customers love this unadulterated honeycomb. The second box, which I placed on top of the Ross rounds super, was a box of drawn comb with a bit of honey still present. (Drawn comb is honeycomb made during a prior honey flow, which alleviates a lot of work for the bees because they don't have to make all that wax.) The loose honey present in the top box acts like bee magnet sending the bees into an ecstatic tizzy. Once I replaced the covers, the bees began to explore these two new floors of their home. I know from my 20+ years of beekeeping that the bees will move their currently-stored honey up from the brood comb below, thus releasing more area for the Queen to lay eggs.

Making wax is a lot of work and bees are generally lazy. Despite their reputation for being hard workers, bees don't seem to want to work any harder than they must. (In this regard, bees are not much different from us humans.) Bees on the move from one home to the other expect to make wax, however, because after all they are carrying honey with them and they know that the honey must go somewhere in a new home. What if they had selected a hollow in a tree for a home? They would have had to make wax honeycomb in which to store their treasure. You can see why my waiting hive with drawn comb appeared very attractive to the scouts. When CM and I spied the bees from the kitchen window, the scout bees had already determined my vacant beehive was the best place to go.

Bees are also very OCD (again, not much different from some of us humans). They prefer to work from the bottom up, like a mason building a chimney. The Ross round super with its thin wafers of wax foundation not drawn out (thus not thick enough to hold honey) vexes the bees, placed as it is between two boxes of drawn comb. By sticking my super of Ross rounds between the stored honey below and the empty, drawn-out super above, I'm encouraging the bees to do what they prefer not to do—make wax in the Ross rounds. Because they are sort of OCD, it goes against their grain to use the top box without drawing comb in the middle box. Tricky, eh? Sometimes the bees fall for my tricks to get them to do what I want. Most times, however, they do not.

When I was about eight-years-old, I ate my first comb honey. There is nothing quite like the nearly orgasmic sensation of biting into the soft wax, releasing warm, sweet honey. Oh, my! My mouth waters as I write, reliving that first taste of honeycomb. After that encounter with comb honey, I promised myself that I would keep bees myself someday. Now, I often steal a frame of honey from the hive after a spring honey flow so I can engorge on the freshly-filled beeswax, much like the bees engorge on their stores before taking flight on the way to a new home.

I don't know yet which of my neighbors to thank for my new miracle hive. One doesn't want to be too obvious about having captured a wayward swarm, as one probably wouldn't be in much of a hurry to return a neighbor's stray chicken if one wanted fresh eggs. Someone near us an inexperienced beekeeper failed to note the signs that her hive was about to swarm. The blessings of Mother Nature are many and varied!

Miracle swarm of honeybees on the way to my empty hive.

June 20, 2017

Sam Vireo

Today it is 85° with 75% humidity. It would be oppressing except that I'm cool and comfortable under the apple tree, thrilled to be observing my new honeybees steadily bringing in nectar. Lord, what a wonderful sight! I can hardly contain my joy. My soul seems to expand upward and float off toward the pond.

Two frontal systems—a hot humid one from the south and a cool one that slipped down from Canada—are fighting over central Maine today. Thunderstorms, hail, and heavy rains are forecast for later, when the fronts collide in earnest.

A phoebe calls out from the other side of the pond. "Phoebe. Phoe-be!" When she receives no reply, phoebe moves further into the woods to try her luck there. My mysterious warbler, which I recently discovered is not a warbler at all, sings out his regular four notes. A bullfrog *rhuums.*

Yesterday while reading *Audubon* magazine, I discovered an article about the red-eyed vireo, a migrating songbird that the author suggests has a melody by which one can begin to learn how to identify bird songs. Sure enough, I checked out the red-eyed vireo bird call at the Cornell University website and lo and behold!

I heard the familiar song of my mysterious "warbler," which song has nearly driven me crazy over the past two years. I don't know that I feel much differently now than before I knew he was not a warbler but a red-eyed vireo. For I feel I have gotten to know my songster as he himself, a personality in his own right, and attaching a label to my friend suddenly makes him seem more removed from me and our relationship formal and sterile. I think I will just call my old friend "Sam Vireo."

The apple branches above my head are filled with tiny green globes. There will be apples this fall! The natural pollinators did their job well it seems.

Speaking of natural pollinators, the wild bee nest box now has more than a dozen tubes filled and mudded off. Even as I write I see the butt end of a bee—black with bright gold stripes—sticking out at me. The owner of the butt, which is larger than what Cranberry Man calls a sweat bee (one of his favorite natural pollinators on the cranberries, about the size of a mayfly nymph) is busily packing something into the end of one of the hollow tubes. Apparently, she has already laid her eggs and is now finishing up the job.

We have been getting in some of our first-cut hay. Last year first-cut was all we got due to the drought. As a result, we reduced our Scottish Highland herd from 30 animals down to 16. About half of the 14 we sold for breeding stock and the other half we sold as beef. This year the grass has been plentiful—and so has the rain been. We need three to four days of sun and wind to cut, dry, and bale hay and as we are going into a rainy period it looks as though we won't be haying again until after the 4th of July.

My mother's committal service is July 1st. It will be good to get that over with. I will feel more at peace when her ashes have been returned to Mother Earth: "Ashes to ashes, dust to dust." In the meantime, I have the sweet fragrance of the locust blooms; the cheerful, busy activity of my new honeybees; and Sam Vireo's song to sustain me.

Unfortunately, I also learned whilst discovering Sam's identity that his main food is the tent caterpillar! Now I regret destroying all those tent caterpillar nests, since without his major food source here on the farm Sam might be tempted to leave me. It would serve me right if—by my heavy-handedness and long-standing hatred of tent caterpillars—I lost the company of one of my new dear companions. (Funny how the most annoying of our friends can somehow become our dearest.) I must remember next year not to be so determined in my destruction of tent caterpillar nests. For everything God creates has a purpose.

And now the annoying no-see-ums have found me and begun to nibble. What's up with that, God?

June 22, 2017

The Cows

It is such a relief today to sit in my lawn chair and put my feet up. I don't know how it happens, but Cranberry Man and I both end up running around like chickens with our heads cut off in summer. (Slight pause here as I reposition my chair because the hot sun came out from behind the clouds and beat down upon my exposed legs.)

I lie here with my arms on the armrests and my legs up, breathing deeply, trying to catch my breath. It seems as though I've been run, run, running lately: haying; weeding and replanting my vegetable garden; weed whacking the fence line; selling, packing, and delivering meat; doing laundry and house cleaning; watering the plants; working belatedly on my new novel; AND making sure everyone is fed, CM, me, the mother-in-law, the songbirds and hummingbirds.

Phew! No wonder I'm tired. I deserve a rest. So … a rest I will now take!

Later the same afternoon

I enjoyed an hour's repose, dozing off and on while listening to the mournful cooing of the doves and to the breeze rustle the leaves of the trees. Usually, the doves coo in the evening, but today, perhaps because the clouds have moved in and the sky has darkened ominously, the doves are crooning earlier.

A blue darning needle hovers in front of the beehive, as though trying to peer in and see what the bees are up to. After 15-20 seconds of spying on them, she zips away.

The honeybees have been busy bringing in nectar from the blackberry blossoms and the remaining black locust blooms. The gusty wind has shorn those gangly trees of much of their delicate blossoms. The blooms cover the ground like white rose petals tossed by a flower girl before the bride.

The back lawn, which CM mowed yesterday, smells spicy, like the scent of thyme. I'm wondering if he didn't accidentally get too close to my herb garden, but I haven't had the courage to check yet.

Sam, my red-eyed vireo, is quiet today, as is Mr. Chippy. I haven't heard or seen Walter the tree frog since our encounter in the pocket of the maple tree. Occasionally I hear a loud chirping near where I am and my heart leaps in excitement. I eagerly look around—until I remember that I changed the ringer on my phone from a favorite song to that of the chirping call of the gray tree frog. This unusual ringer is a gift from a herpetologist friend I follow on Twitter.

Cranberry Man disapproves of the tree frog ringtone because it is so realistic. He doesn't like the idea of a frog in the house. Yesterday my phone rang while I was at the dentist's office and you should have seen the look on the face of dental hygienist. "What kind of a bird is that?" she asked. "It's a tree frog," I replied. "Oh? What kind of a bird is that?" I took the opportunity to enlighten her that a tree frog is not a bird but a herp (short for herptile, from the Greek word "herpein," which means "to creep"). I wondered how she could be so ignorant. But then I thought about how many things there are in the natural world about which I am ignorant and felt ashamed of myself.

Now Mr. Chippy has taken up a post in the pine tree behind me. He is chattering loudly—pausing—chattering again, as though he's on the phone with a friend or his mate. "I'm going to be late for dinner, dear. Don't wait for me." "What's taking you so long?" "There's a raven guarding the bird feeders—a large black one on the grape arbor just waiting for me to do something stupid. I must wait for him to move on." Etc. Etc.

There is indeed a big fat raven on my grape arbor. As I watch him, the raven spreads his huge black wings and flaps off somewhere over the pond. Mr. Chippy is now free to make his regular run for bird seed.

I have a pair of ravens on the farm—whom I've christened Romeo and Juliet—that have somehow made their way into my new novel. I'm almost up to 60,000 words. Only 20,000-25,000 left to go. Not sure how many chapters that will be. I'll just write until the book is done. I hope I know when that occurs, and stop writing.

Sam Vireo sends out a few half-hearted melodic notes. He's closer to the head of the pond today, closer, no doubt, to those tent caterpillars in my mother-in-law's trees.

CM made a run to Charleston this morning to pick up the meat from the two animals he took to slaughter last week. We now have three freezers full of beef. I have several meat deliveries scheduled for tomorrow and a pick-up coming later today.

The longer we are in farming—and the older we get—the more distasteful raising animals for beef becomes. I remember how as my uncle got older it became more difficult for him to kill a deer during hunting season. Something like that is going on for us. I'll be sixty-one in August and CM is sixty-six.

When I was twenty, I visited a beef feedlot in Colorado where a friend was working. The conditions under which the cows were kept and force-fed with grain—which necessitated huge doses of antibiotics to keep the animals alive long enough to fatten for slaughter—were so horrific I didn't eat beef for nearly a decade. When I did return to beef, I sourced my meat from local farms where I knew the animals were raised humanely and without grain. (Cows are ruminants and the overuse of grain produces in their multiple stomachs runaway bacteria that makes them sick.) About ten years ago CM—a long-time hunter—decided he was tired of shooting and butchering deer for our meat. I had long wanted to raise cows, but knew I couldn't do it alone. When I suggested we raise beef animals, CM allowed it might not be a bad idea, especially as it would put all his old family pastures and fields back into production. We started our herd with four cows, using artificial insemination to breed the bovines in the early years to increase the genetic diversity of the herd. Then we began raising our own bulls. When we decided to reduce our herd last year during the drought, we sold our gentle herd bull Merlin of Troy to a couple from Connecticut. They fell in love with Merlin and wanted to show him (Merlin is registered with the American Highland Cattle Association) and his offspring. So, Merlin will enjoy some more good years before ending up at the slaughter house, where almost all bovines end their lives.

Now we are down to around 16 animals, mostly our breeding herd and a few young bulls we are raising for beef. We're keeping an eye on the future, which draws closer every year, the future in which we will not have to work so hard and sweat so much. That eventually means a future without cows, but hopefully we will end with three freezers full of meat, so I'll never have to buy commercially-raised beef again.

Mr. Chippy has just popped out from one of his nests, which is under a bunch of dried leaves and twigs. This particular nest looks like a miniature beaver hut. He pops out, stands up on his haunches, and looks me right in the eye. (We are only about eight feet apart.) Then he bounds past me in my chair and scoots under the pallet upon which the beehive sits. (The beehive is only about four feet away from me today.) He checks things out under the pallet, where he's stored plenty of sunflower seeds for winter, and then sneaks out the front door. When he exits his winter storage area, Mr. Chippy runs up onto the heart-shaped granite bird bath, which is on a pile of rocks next to the beehive and which I keep filled with fresh water for the bees. My pint-sized friend drinks his fill. He is almost too cute for words.

Mr. Chippy is precocious, too. I've discovered that he uses my presence to his advantage. He obviously seems to know that when I'm sitting here that I—a large, two-legged beast—am the apex predator in the neighborhood. When I'm under the apple tree his natural predators (except for the ravens Romeo and Juliet) are wary of coming too close to me, thus making the area clear for Mr. Chippy. As a result, rather than take his circuitous route around the edges of the lawn thru the tall grass and leaves, Mr. Chippy makes a beeline for the bird feeder. In effect, my presence here enables him to make many more trips to the bird feeder in a shorter period.

I hear one of our young calves mooing anxiously from across the pond in Pasture 1. He must have become separated from his mother. The calf moos again, and I hear a faint answering moo in response from the far end of the pond. Mum has told him to come to her—she's not coming to him (she's likely feeding on lush green grass). I hear branches break as the youngster excitedly races thru the woods to rejoin his mother and the herd.

The sun comes out again. The air heats up. The scent of thyme intensifies. The thyme and the smell of freshly-mown grass act as intoxicants. I feel light-headed and drowsy. Surely, it must be time for another doze?

Some of our cows and calves relaxing in the field next to the pond.

June 24, 2017

Surprise Amarylis in the Garden (A Gift from Mom)

This morning the air was humid, and then it rained heavily. Since the storm passed, however, we have been enjoying the sun and some fresh Canadian air. I know I should mow the front lawn now that the grass has dried out, but I don't budge.

I'm so exhausted today I don't intend to write long, either. I need to put my feet up, inhale the sweet scent of Mother Nature, and relax. I've worked myself to the bone over the past three days unpacking, weighing, organizing, and sorting and storing the meat from the two animals we sent to slaughter; packing up meat orders to go; and delivering the orders to Unity, Sabattus, and Westbrook.

From Westbrook, I drove up to Norway to check on my mother's headstone. It's my job to ensure that the stone—a lovely and interesting piece of charcoal-colored granite that Mom selected years before she passed—is set on its base and is affixed with a brass plaque stating Mother's name, birth and death dates. Of the four of us kids, I'm the one who volunteered (I guess) to handle the burial and related particulars. I want to ensure that the stone is ready for Mother's committal service next Saturday.

Mr. Chippy suddenly darts out from beneath the beehive and hops over to my blue delphinium, which is in full and glorious bloom. He disappears beneath a pile of leaves there, with which I've composted the plant.

A yellow swallowtail flutters past. My honeybees zip in from gathering nectar and pile up in a traffic jam on the landing board.

Here comes Mr. Chippy back again. Well, I know where he's been! His cheeks are puffed out as though he has mumps. He's obviously been visiting my bird feeders, which I filled this morning. I also cleaned and filled both of my hummingbird feeders because they were both empty. Everybody is hungry!

Mr. Chippy and I have become good friends. He still keeps an eye on me as I sit here, not fearfully, but curiously, as though wondering what I am writing. If he only knew how much is about him!

Cranberry Man has just driven into the driveway. He doesn't see me sitting here under the apple tree, thanks to the tall, thick screen of blackberry bushes. I can peek thru the gaps in the bushes enough to determine who's coming up our gravel driveway. If it's someone I want to avoid I simply remain quiet and let them pound on my door. My house, like my phone, is for my convenience, not theirs. Thanks to my age—and my liberation from "should do's" and "ought to do's" that resulted from my mother's death—I no longer feel obliged to jump up and make myself available to every Tom, Dick, and Harry who drops by, usually wanting something.

When I arrived in Norway, I discovered that my mother's stone was not quite done. The stonemason promised it would be finished and set in Mom's family's plot by July 1st (the date of the committal service). I hope so, because it would be awkward standing in the middle of the cemetery surrounded by Mother's friends and family and have neither her body (she was cremated) nor her gravestone to mourn by.

I am leading the committal service, having been trained for the ministry at Bangor Theological Seminary. I keep telling people the service is going to be "very short," mostly because we've already had the funeral back in the spring, but also because I don't want to make it long. I'll be reading the funeral service from my Minister's Service Book and Mom's dear friend Heather Pierson will be singing *a capella* "The Pennesseewassee Song" that Mother loved. Just thinking of those beautiful notes soaring like white doves released into the air makes the hair on my neck and arms stand up.

When I was cleaning Mom's basement five or six weeks ago, I noticed she had flower bulbs set aside for spring planting. Thinking that the dry, dirty bulbs were gladiolas and dahlias, two of my mother's favorite tender flowers, I brought them home and planted the bulbs in the far side of my vegetable garden, which I'm slowly turning into a perennial bed. The dahlia bulbs were not dahlias, but amaryllis. Surprise! (Obviously, I'm not very good at identifying bulbs.) Now I have a gorgeous blood-red amaryllis blooming alongside prosaic green and yellow wax beans. Earlier the wind snapped off one side of the two-headed amaryllis bloom and the stem was too short to place in a vase, so before I sat down, I placed the blossom into the heart-shaped pink granite bird bath. That water was supposed to be for the honeybees, but I rarely see them drink there. Instead, Mr. Chippy uses the bird bath as his private water supply. He has hopped up twice since I've been sitting here. Now he is perched on the edge of the pink granite, his black-striped back to me, as though miffed at the red bloom floating in his water. He hops down, slightly disgusted, without taking a drink.

A robin flies low over the lawn and then rises up to land in the oak tree above me. My friend Sam Vireo sends out a tired, half-hearted call. He should be tired! Sam V. starts serenading us loudly around 4 a.m.—as soon as daylight begins to creep around the darkness of the night. CM groans when he hears him and twists a pillow around his ears or puts his earplugs in.

The pond smells like fresh lake water today. My mock-orange bush is sending out bursts of sweet-smelling orange scent, too. I have never seen the mock-orange more glorious than today. Two ruby-throated hummingbirds have been fighting over the shrub's antique white blossoms.

Walter the gray tree frog has been silent today. He, too, should be tuckered out. He and his brethren sounded like squabbling monkeys all night. They only quit fighting over the female gray tree frogs early this morning when Sam V. awoke and began singing.

I have a scribbled note on my gardening calendar to check the wild bee nest box tomorrow and see if the mystery bee eggs are hatched. I checked today and the end of the tube in which she laid her eggs is still mudded off. The butt of a wild bee was sticking out one of the other hollows, though. Not sure what she was doing in there, but I assume it has something to do with the propagation of her species. Pretty much sexual reproduction is all that is going on this time of year on the farm.

A friend of mine owns a native pollinator sanctuary and I asked her to send me some information on Maine's wild bees, which she did. This is the summer I will learn more about our native pollinators.

A stray chipmunk (not Mr. Chippy) is making that annoying clucking noise in the back of his throat. The sound emanates from beneath the beehive on the pallet, leading me to suspect that its owner is Mrs. Chippy, whom I've not yet met. Perhaps she is talking to their offspring? I thought Mr. Chippy was quite a busy boy. If he's as busy with the ladies as he is stealing my sunflower seed, he's quite a Lothario.

A songbird twitters from the treetop. A car rushes by out on Route 9. This is the way life should be lived—hanging out in the cool shade under the apple tree with all my summer friends.

Mom's amaryllis bloom in Mr. Chippy's water dish.

June 26, 2017

Sharing the Road with Our Fellow Creatures

A hairy woodpecker was high-speed nailing in one of the tall maples when I arrived beneath the apple tree today. Now he has stopped—woodpecker interruptus.

I should be tedding hay, but Cranberry Man accidentally bent the three-point-hitch whilst backing the tedder out of the barn. He then spent the next three to four hours attempting to repair it, machinist that he is by trade. The new part, he says, would cost over $300. I don't know how anyone can afford to farm these days if they don't have CM's mechanical abilities. I see now that he has gone out to ted the hay field across the road—and rise to go do my duty.

Ten minutes later

I walked over, ear protectors and sunglasses in hand, but Cranberry Man waved me away. (Tedding or turning the cut hay to facilitate the drying is one of my designated tasks on the farm.) No doubt CM wants to ensure the repaired hitch is working correctly and that it doesn't fly apart in the middle of me tedding. As a result, I have more time to repose.

A drone (male honeybee) is now buzzing around me, checking me out. I do seem to irritate the drones as I am so close to the hive. This afternoon I'm about eight feet away. The worker bees, however, just keep on doing their thing, which is work, something the drones avoid. The drones spend their time flying around looking for virgin queens to impregnate. I'm not thinking they will have much luck scoring in this neighborhood, which might explain this drone's evident frustration.

I've been reflecting about the creatures with whom we share this beautiful spot on earth. In particular, I've realized how hard it must be for them to live with us—to work their lives around us—as the dominant or keystone species. Yesterday when I was out making meat deliveries, I was suddenly awakened to the large number of roadkill I drove past. I counted two dead porcupines, a chipmunk, a gray squirrel, and a baby woodchuck. Yesterday evening, after returning from my meat deliveries, CM and I went out for supper. On the drive to the restaurant, I counted one dead raccoon, a porcupine, and two very little woodchucks. So sad! These creatures are not trying to commit suicide. They are simply attempting to cross the road, our domain, but also theirs.

I recall the one and only time I ever killed anything with a vehicle. When I was a teenager, one night I hit a cat while racing home late from play practice. I was speeding, trying to make my 11 p.m. curfew, going 65-70 MPH on a curvy, country road posted at 45. A neighbor's cat darted into the path of my headlights, as cats do, mesmerized by the powerful light. I heard a thud as I hit him. I wavered about what to do. (I was late, and a teenager, remember.) Finally, thanks to an active conscience instilled in me by my mother, I turned the car around and went back to examine the calico cat, which was dead, of course, with a broken neck.

Now, the cat belonged to one of the poorer families in the neighborhood, one would almost call them from the "wrong side of the tracks." These people lived in a little red shack overrun with kids, junk, dead automobiles in various stages of decay, and a killer dog. But I screwed up my courage and despite the late hour and the blackness of the night, I stumbled over the junk and knocked on the front door. The killer dog inside awoke and began barking furiously, awakening the rest of the household, to whom I was soon confessing my sin. I carried the cat's body in my arms and the father of the tribe (all of which were huddled at the door) took the feline from me and showed real grief at the loss. Likewise, there was similar bemoaning from the various tribe members. Only the dog seemed pleased at the demise of the cat, stopping barking long enough to smile.

I felt awful. The father was very gracious to me, however. Even though I was the cat killer, he thanked me for coming to tell them. He was especially grateful I'd removed the feline from the middle of the road so that its carcass wouldn't be run over again and again. The father said they would bury the cat in the morning and told the tribe to return to bed. I didn't see what he did with the dead feline, for I was already making my exit around the junk on the front lawn, having done my duty.

Fortunately, my parents were understanding when I told them why I was late that night. I received no punishment, my parents probably thinking I had been punished enough by my own conscience. There was never a moment when they doubted my story, either. The cat's blood was all over my clothing.

After that episode, I slowed down when driving. I also began watching for my fellow creatures of the Earth, who often frequent the roadside. Many, many times I've captured green cat eyes in my headlights—or deer eyes—and I immediately brake, knowing how vulnerable the animal is to the blinding light. I also switch from high beams to low beams, which often releases the critter from my headlight's vice grip.

Also, after that day, my parents never gave me a curfew again. I asked my mother once years after I had left home, why this was so, especially since my older sister was usually given a firm deadline, a time by which time she should be home. "We trusted you," Mom said. And that was that. So … you see what a sensitive conscience will net you?

Now, Phoebe is calling out her name. There is no reply. She keeps calling. Has she lost her mate? Or is she teaching her young ones how to talk?

Robin Adair (my new nickname for my friendly robin) is on my shit list. He's been visiting our strawberry patch, which is over by my husband's workshop, helping himself to the ripe berries. Robin did this last year, too. I wouldn't mind sharing if Robin Adair wasn't so greedy! He takes one or two bites out of a lush, red strawberry—always the biggest and best berry, of course. He hauls the berry out of the patch to the straw on the edge, takes his bite or two, and then abandons the berry as though it wasn't good enough for him. Robin Adair then promptly selects another juicy red strawberry and repeats the process.

CM is very angry with Robin. He rose at 4 a.m. today to go out and pick two quarts of strawberries before Robin Adair could get them. I went over a little while ago and discovered that CM must have missed one or two for Robin A. had been there again and left his tell-tale calling card in the straw.

The barometric pressure has fallen suddenly as the menacing clouds push in, obscuring the sun. My honeybees are happy because the low barometric pressure forces the nectar in flowers further out in the stem, making the nectar more readily available to the short-tongued bees. Hundreds of honeybees are now bouncing in the air in front of the hive (orienting themselves), new foragers liberated from cleaning the hive who will shortly zip off on their maiden flights. I'm wondering what nectar crop is active since the blackberries and black locust blooms have passed by. It could be the bedstraw, an invasive flowering weed introduced by the Maine Department of Transportation years ago and whose long-flowing tufts of white hair are ruining hayfields throughout Maine, including ours.

CM is on the four-wheeler, calling to the cows. He must be moving them into another pasture. Behind me on the South Mitchell Road an awful noise has started up. It is most likely our neighbor who owns a used granite business and is always loading or unloading a pile of old field stones, well covers, stoop stones, grist mill grinders, and more.

CM just rode over on the ATV to tell me what pasture he moved the cows into. (We use rotational grazing and I keep a record of our pastures.) He also informed me of the time—4:50 p.m.! Where do the hours go?

I dashed into the house to put the potatoes and chicken in the oven and to phone and inform the mother-in-law about dinner. When I returned to collect my things from the lawn chair, the hairy woodpecker had begun hammering again. The birds chirped. The bees buzzed.

I so wanted to linger longer under the apple tree, but, once again, duty calls. I need to pick and clean the spinach for supper, cut up the strawberries, and bake the biscuits for strawberry shortcake. There is never enough time on the farm! I snatched these precious moments today only because the tedder was down. I have so much more I wanted to write, but it will have to wait for another day.

Cranberry Man on the ATV.

June 29, 2017

Summer "Drops" and May Sarton

I'm sad to report that many of the little green apples have dropped from my tree. I set my chair up today on a bed of them. As they lay scattered on the ground they looked like solid pea-green shooter marbles. It is very windy today, but sunny and about 80°. The wind is from the SW, bringing us in some bad weather in addition to the apple drops, I fear.

I had hoped the drops were just Mother Nature's regular pruning—summer drops, as we call them. But I examined the large apple branch above my head, which is most of what's left of the old apple tree, and I don't see many fruits remaining. One more apple has dropped since I sat down, plunking into my lap as I was writing.

My honeybees are moderately busy gathering nectar, although they are having a bit of difficulty managing their return flights to the beehive as the gusty wind keeps blowing them off course. I hear the pinging of my wind chime that hangs in the ornamental crab out in front of the house. The wind is carrying the steady, tinkling sound on its back. The tinkling is like the bell of an ice cream truck; such a thrilling sound!

I've done some research on my mystery bee and suspect she is a type of mason bee. Masons get their name because they lay their eggs in hollow tubes (in this case, in my bee condominium) and then plug the ends of the tubes with mud and other substances, such as chewed up pithy grasses and vegetation. The dozen or so hollows she has filled are still mudded up. No more have been added. Today when I arrived a gadabout mayfly was checking out the wild bee nest box. But Ms. Mayfly was just curious. After inspecting the Apoidea, she flew over and landed on me. I kept waving her away, but she returned several times. Curious creature!

Mr. Hairy Woodpecker is chirping his loud, one-note chirp down by the pond. A variety of other songbirds are adding their melodies to the mix.

Mother Bluebird has fledged her young. I saw her teaching two of them to fly. The youngsters were poised to take off from the wooden grape arbor. I watched the young birds and they did very well on their maiden flights.

There is a lot of traffic out on Route 9 today. We are approaching the 4th of July holiday weekend and everyone is busy going and coming or getting ready to go or come.

My mother's committal service is Saturday at 11 a.m. in Norway Pine Grove Cemetery in Paris, Maine. I'm about as ready as I ever will be to finally lay her to rest.

The wind dies down for a moment. A drone zips by, buzzing loudly like a big, fat bumblebee. The air is becoming more humid, as though preparing for the rain, which the wind is bearing northward.

I inhale deeply and lean back in my chair. I am tired. So tired! I seem to be nipped at continuously from all sides, as though someone turned a pack of dogs loose on me. However, I'm hiding behind the blackberry bushes—under the apple tree—with a good book, May Sarton's, *The Bridge of Years.*

I have been reading May Sarton, the New Hampshire (and later Maine) poet and novelist, a lot lately, having discovered some of her books, including her wonderful journal *Plant Dreaming Deep*, among my mother's collection. Once I found her books, I remembered how much Mom loved May Sarton. I never read Miss Sarton's work until now. Now, however, I can't seem to get enough of her. I'm falling under the poet's spell even as my mother did thirty or forty years ago. As a result, I'm not coming out from behind the blackberry bushes no matter who comes up the driveway!

July 3, 2017

Mason Bees at Work

Today two different mason bees are busily working away in my wild bee nest box. I have a new bee book (two books, actually, but only one with me today under the apple tree) and when I'm done scribbling in this journal, I'm going to attempt to identify my new tenants. One (the smaller bee) is using green grass and/or other green vegetation to mud off the ends of her tubes. She's currently disgorging this green stuff, which she neatly packs into the end of the tube. The larger bee, which resembles an anorexic yellow jacket, has now disappeared inside one of the larger tubes and is presumably laying her eggs.

I get up to investigate again and see that a smaller bee has now disappeared inside another hollow. What a breeding hotel we are running here! Unable to resist the siren's call of curiosity, I resort immediately to my bee book.

My wild bee nest box, with some of the tubes filled.

An hour later

Well, so much for good intentions. As I perused my new bee book, attempting to discern what type of mason bees my visitors are, my eyelids became very heavy and I dozed off. I'm exhausted after two days of physical and emotional stress from my mother's committal service. Plus, the wind rustling the leaves of the trees combined with the gentle cooing of the mourning doves was very relaxing.

Now I lay back in my chair with my feet up, my couch quilt (which my mother sewed) wrapped around me, the west wind having a bit of a chill today. I'm enjoying the scents of the mown grass and tedded hay. There is intermittent chatter from various songbirds and the mourning doves are at it again. Sam Vireo has started back up, too. (I think we dozed off together.) He is singing from the top of one of the black locust trees over by my husband's workshop and the strawberry beds. I didn't sweep for tent caterpillar beds over in that area, so he's likely getting lucky.

This morning, I tedded the cut hay in the three fields Cranberry Man had mowed across the road from the house. It took me a while to ted because he had worked hard over the past few days when I was gone to Norway to repair the tines on the tedder (which resemble talons), as well as the arms that hold them altogether. Anyway, CM was like a new mother with her baby, hardly letting me out of his sight so anxious was he that I might bend the tines. "Stay away from the woods!" he called, running up next to me on his ATV. He buzzed around me worse than a wasp. Then he buzzed off.

My blood pressure began to rise when I saw him head my way again. However, CM zipped up, shut the ATV off, removed his helmet, and said some sweet words to me on the tractor. Then the sun came out and the joy returned. He told me I was doing a "good job" and then buzzed off home and left me tedding the hay in peace.

Hay waiting to be tedded (taken from my John Deere tractor).

July 5, 2017

Death of Mr. Chippy

I have only 45 minutes before I need to go ted hay, however, I wanted to seek solace under the apple tree because I fear Mr. Chippy is dead. I anxiously scan the short piece of woods running down to the pond, checking for my little friend in his usual haunts. Alas, alas! He is not to be seen nor heard. I even cleaned and refreshed the water in the granite bird bath hoping to tempt Mr. Chippy out of hiding for a cool drink on this hot day. But to no avail.

Cranberry Man told me casually yesterday when we were checking the strawberries that he had found a dead chipmunk laying on the straw that morning. My heart jumped in fear and I inquired about the particulars. I knew (or suspected, anyway) that my little friend had made his way over to the strawberry bed, for I had picked a few ripe berries lately with telltale chipmunk teeth marks in them. Apparently, Mr. Chippy became a little too cocky in his wanderings. Either that or his time was up. CM said there were no obvious bite marks or wounds on my little friend. He suspects the culprit is a stray black-and-white cat that's been making the rounds of the neighborhood over the past few years. I told CM the next time he saw the cat to shoot it!

I can't express how keenly I feel the loss of my small friend. Sitting here is not the same without Mr. Chippy's cheerful comings and goings. I feel lonely and alone now. I have my honeybees to keep me company, true. They are very active today, humming happily. I also have the activity in the wild bee nest box to engage me. But these delights by themselves do not make up for the loss of Mr. Chippy—his exuberance, his lively chatter, his silly antics all to some deep chipmunk purpose—and so I miss him!

Sad. Very sad.

And now Cranberry Man has come to tell me it's time to ted the hay. For the first time ever, I'm glad to leave my spot here under the apple tree.

July 7, 2017

Mr. Chippy's Children and the Woods

Today it is overcast, gloomy, and the air is very oppressive. It feels as though the intensity of the day will slowly build and culminate in a thunderstorm. My garden needs the rain—and we put our last round bale of hay under cover yesterday—so I look forward to the dousing.

A green frog *gunks* from the pond. The birds are chirping overhead, calling gaily to one another. The bees are very active, so I know the barometric pressure has fallen. There is a damp scent of fecundity issuing from the woods and pond today, reminiscent of deep woods in summertime.

When I first sat down, I was greeted by the usual chirping of a chipmunk. My heart failed to ignite, however, for I know my dear friend Mr. Chippy is indeed dead. However, he has left behind two reminders of himself. Two days ago—not long after I penned my previous entry—I spied a chipmunk on one of our bird feeders. Then, my heart leapt with hope and excitement. Mr. Chippy! Mr.

Chippy is alive! When I moved to the window to check, the chipmunk leapt down and joined a second on the ground. They played with each other for several seconds, until I bent closer to look and they darted off into the safety of the tall grass. Now, Mr. Chippy would not have run away—he would have stood his ground, so sure of me he was. He would have stared back at me boldly from the bird feeder (as he often did when I caught sight of him from the window), his bright black eyes telegraphing: "I know who you are and I know you won't hurt me!"

No, my visitors were immature chipmunks, Mr. Chippy's children, reared by their mother in the safety of their burrow. Now, being teenagers (in chipmunk time), their mom has kicked them out and these two must find their own territory. Chipmunks are very territorial. I've read that mature males often move on and leave their old territory to their offspring; however, I don't think Mr. Chippy meant to "move on" in quite the way he did. Anyway, it appears as though one of Mr. Chippy's offspring has taken up shop in this small piece of woods between me and the pond. I have something to look forward to, as I wonder whether he (or she!) will befriend me as Mr. Chippy did. Will the young chipmunk(s) learn to accept me? To understand I mean them no harm? (And, in fact, that I am the one who fills the bird feeders!) Will they find the stash of black oil sunflower seeds that their dad has squirrelled away under the beehive pallet? There must be five pounds under there, at least!

Now, I hear a new squeaking and soft chirping. I lay back in my chair gazing up at the soft green canopy of leaves from whence the chirping comes. I see small black bodies darting to and fro between the trees and realize the sound is that of Mr. and Mrs. Hairy Woodpecker teaching their offspring how to fly. What a wonderful yet awful world they have been born into! I wonder what these young birds think and feel as they take their first flights into the richly-green floating garden. The tops of the trees sway gently back and forth in the southern breeze. One of the young lands about 15 feet up the side of a tall maple—so tall I can't see its top, rising as it does up and above all the other trees in this magical grove. Baby

H.W.P. clings to the side of the scarred and serrated gray bark—smattered all over with light green patches of fungus and dark moss—as though wondering what she is supposed to do next. Just when I think she's going to "get it" and begin pecking for bugs, she lifts her wings and drops a bit, fluttering frantically. She finally makes her way to a branch in a poplar tree about twenty feet away. She did it! She flew on her own.

My baby chipmunks have gone to ground. I hear only an occasional tell-tale squeaking (and that faraway) as though they are checking for the presence of other chippies in that area in preparation for claiming the territory. I hope at least one of them returns to my neck of the woods under the apple tree so that I might monitor their progress. I've read recently that chipmunks can live 8-9 years, but average only 2 in the wild. I think Mr. Chippy was at least 2-years-old for I'm sure he was the chipmunk that befriended me last summer.

I realize now that I haven't written enough about this grove of trees. I wouldn't be sitting here if it weren't for the presence of these tall leafy creatures. The one spindly, gnarled apple branch that leans out from the woods trying to stay alive hasn't enough of its small, tapered leaves to provide me with complete shade.

I have largely ignored the woods because most of the time my chair is facing toward the blackberries and house (or toward the Apoidea), so I can keep an eye out for whomever might come up the driveway. We get very few friends who visit, like we used to in the old days when folks stopped in to say "hello" and just chat, leaning on the sides of their trucks. Folks in the old days (and I'm talking 40-50 years ago now) were more neighborly. Now, most all the people who make their way up our driveway want something and it's often a tricky thing for me to figure out whether it's worthwhile to break my repose and venture out from my hiding place. Visitors are always startled to see me emerge from what has looked like an empty back lawn; however, they can't see beyond the tall, thick mass of blackberries and the bowed apple branch beneath which I park my chair. Like Mr. Chippy, I like to hide.

Today I have turned my chair around so my back is to the driveway and I'm gazing into this lovely stretch of woods. The cows start grazing around the pond in the spring just as the sweet green shoots are pushing up. There isn't enough grass to go around, so the mature cows put the horns to the younger ones, pushing them continuously ahead of the herd. The heifers and young steers find themselves on the backside of the pond, the side closest to the house, where there is only the fence and a narrow strip of trees between them and the water. With big cows pushing along behind them, the young ones have no place to go but into this piece of woods and sometimes I hear the branches snapping and cracking as they move forward breaking trail. The big cows rarely follow them, because there is no grass in the woods—and they aren't stupid.

The young animals emerge into this "wilderness," a triangular-shaped area about half the size of a football field. The first point in the triangle is the path from the pond; the second point is near where I'm sitting (where the north and east fence lines come together); and the third point is over by the back of the barn. Because the mature cows don't follow them here, our young Scottish Highlands consider this their own playground. They wind the small branches of the pines and poplar around the tree, using the branches as combs until the branches snap. Then the heifers and steers use the broken ends as scratching posts, often rubbing their butts up against the sharp point until there is nothing left of the branch but a scar where the branch used to be (and not much hair left on their butts, either). While they are at it (combing and scratching) the youngsters stretch their necks up into the tree, looking like hairy red giraffes, nibbling at the succulent green foliage. (These cows will eat just about anything.) As a result, this little piece of woods is branch-free from about 8-10 feet up, thus offering a clear field of vision down the sloping hill to the pond.

The upper bodies of the tall trees sway in the breeze. They resemble seductive hula dancers, slightly bent over, their long hair like grass skirts swaying in time with the music of the birds and tree frogs.

A thick brown layer of leaves blankets most of this piece of woods. The leaves offered Mr. Chippy plenty of hiding opportunities. How he must have stood out in the strawberry patch! (Again, I told Cranberry Man to shoot that cat, which he's seen a second time near the strawberries.) I'm afraid Mr. Chippy was too bold for his own good. He might have lived another few years if he had stayed closer to home, but the sweet delights of the strawberries were too much for him. (I'm sure there is a moral in there for us.) I hope Mr. Chippy's offspring elect to stay nearer the woods.

The thick layer of leaves in the woods comes in many interesting shades of brown. (I'm only just beginning to appreciate, as I mature in age, the subtle glories of the color brown.) In addition, the ground is littered with dead branches, mostly the ones broken off by the young cows. In the spring, I often throw weeds or last year's dead vegetation over the fence, so there are piles of dead stalks, which Mr. Chippy also used to his advantage. A few green shoots manage to bravely stake their ground in the woods—several immature maples and poplar trees, no bigger than a young raspberry bush—and a few what we call Boston ferns creeping up from the water's edge.

I still hear lots of soft squeaking but can't tell if it's coming from the ground or the trees. Some mother is no doubt giving her offspring a lecture in "how to live in the Maine woods." A mature bird just made a chuckling noise from a tree down by the pond, perhaps eavesdropping on this interesting lecture and remembering "when."

There are only a couple of dozen mature trees in the woods, three or four lovely and graceful birches; and a stolid burr oak that drops its furry acorns when it's a seed year and offers me plenty of shade. The burr oak reaches high up and has many branches that stretch out over the back lawn looking like outfielders trying to catch a long fly ball. There are also a goodly number of maple trees of all ages mixed in among the other hardwoods. Their tops mingle together although they give each other plenty of space on the ground. Trees keep a respectful distance from one another, and prefer to group with their own kind, I've noticed.

Thru the verdure the summer sunlight tries to wend its way; however, the light ends up being reflected off the leaves, tossed from one shiny green leaf to another. When the light finally filters down to the ground there is little left of its strength and nothing left of the sun's heat, which evaporates into the cool forest. I love the dappled sunlight, even though it occasionally causes me to readjust my baseball cap or move my chair so that I can read without a shard of light poking thru a wormhole in the canopy.

The woods slope down to the pond. Sometimes it appears as though the trees are on the move, walking down to see a duck parade or perhaps to fetch a drink of water. Immature trees line the water's edge. They crowd there like children at a parade. The older, wiser trees remain unmoved up top, knowing that the best place to be is on the high ground. Besides, they are so tall they don't need to be in the front row, they can see everything.

Another *gunk* from the green frog in the pond. (Nine varieties of frogs and toads can be found in Maine and all nine make their home here on the farm.) I have not heard Walter the gray tree frog in his hidey hole in a great while. Now that the hot weather is here (and most of his breeding work is done, I suspect), my friend Walter prefers to remain closer to the water. At night I hear him and his buddies purring and chirping loudly outside our open windows beside the pond. They sound like a bunch of Old Farts gossiping down to the general store. I also occasionally hear the short snore of a pickerel frog, the trill of an American toad (or two), and—one of my favorites—the muffled tapping sound of the mysterious mink frog.

Sam Vireo., that effervescent, tireless singer, has relocated to the other side of the pond, next to my mother-in-law's house. I think again how I destroyed all his food source here by following my destructive tent caterpillar Pest Management Plan (PMP) this spring. Still, upon reflection, I am OK that Sam sings further away and that my young fruit trees have been spared defoliation from the tent caterpillars. The two sour cheery trees have been putting their energy into bearing fruit and are now bursting with unripe, yellow-orange berries. In approximately a week the berries will come into the full, red ripeness of being.

I check my cherry trees every day—if not several times a day—and already have seen where the birds have been checking them, too. I've noted the occasional bite into a cherry where some bird has been checking for ripeness. It is nearly impossible to beat the birds to harvest—they seem to know the exact moment the cherries are ripe. Hopefully, I'll net enough fruit to bake a sour cherry pie (or two) and freeze some berries for winters pies, by which we'll remember the sweetness of this summer day.

The soft squeaking noises I was hearing have stopped. The wind has died down. There is only a hint of lazy movement, nearly soundless, of the leaves in the trees.

The chirping of the birds, the scent of the woods, the heaviness of the air—pregnant with the impending storm—have made my pen slow and my brain all but stop functioning. I feel my brain switch from "reasoning" mode to "being" mode. Shortly, I predict, I will just be—asleep.

The pond as seen through the trees.

July 8, 2017

Removing Honey from the Hive

I must look rather funny sitting here today under the apple tree suited up in my white bee-suit, waiting for the sun to come around so I can remove the honey boxes from my beehive. The wind has picked up, unfortunately, which is not good. When I'm working my hives, I accidentally kill more bees when the wind blows.

I need the direct hot sun to heat up the fume board, a cloth-lined board placed over the top of the hive after I remove the cover. I coat the cloth on the underside of the fume board with formic acid, a natural but nasty smelling liquid the bees hate. As the aluminum on top of the fume board heats up, the smell gets stronger and stronger and the bees—grumbling all the way—gradually move down from the honey supers into the two lower brood boxes allowing me to remove the supers without taking the bees along for the ride. Often, if the hive contains a large swarm of bees, the younger bees will head for the exit, hanging comically on top of one another on the outside of the lower boxes like passengers on a sinking ship.

A woodpecker drills a tree across the pond. He pauses (to eat a bug?) and then drills again. Route 9 is active today, with cars buzzing by as everyone is on a mission to get somewhere, anywhere but where they are. I am grateful to be exactly where I want to be.

The wind lifts the stray strands of my hair that have escaped the ponytail. The breeze carries to my nostrils the faint wet-chimney scent of my dirty bee smoker, which is open and filled with bits of dried, fuzzy red sumac blossoms; dead leaves; and dry cedar fronds waiting to be lighted. My fume board is out on the lawn, aluminum side up, soaking up the sun like a sunbather on the beach. Nearby I hear the crazy laughter of an unknown bird. A pileated woodpecker? That would explain the drilling sound.

I check the top of the beehive again. Some sun is hitting the top, but not enough to work the bees yet. Now, to patiently sit back and wait and enjoy this lovely Saturday morning, one summer in Maine. I wonder when I eat the honey in days to come whether I will remember the dappled sunlight coming thru the trees? Will I think of the graceful shadows of the dancing branches? Robin Adair's particular cheeps? The warm breath of an impending thunderstorm? Or even remember the buzzing and peaceful comings and goings of these hard-working creatures that provide us with such delicious-tasting joy?

My comb honey, packaged for sale.

July 11, 2017

Becky and the Inchworm

A miniature inchworm must have fallen from the apple tree or made its way onto the pillow while it was resting on the ground, for I just spied the tiny creature—no thicker than one of my white hairs—valiantly inching along. I brushed him off into the air, not even caring if he lived or died.

This is the year of death, I guess. Yesterday, Becky, one of my dear friends since elementary school days sent out a group text announcing that she was leaving the VA hospital under the care of hospice. This is the same friend who has battled ovarian cancer for the past two years, who went thru her mother's death only a short while after *my* mother's death. Oh, the world is so hard to live in sometimes that it seems as though we must die to escape the pain!

I'm glad I made the effort to visit Becky in New Hampshire when her mother was dying, for that will probably be the last time I see her. I called her as soon as I received the text and she says she isn't sure she'll be up for company when she gets home from the hospital. She's already begun to detach from the world. I pray she doesn't suffer long.

July 16, 2017

Grateful to Be Alive

The difference between being in the shade and being in the sun is startling today. In the sun, it's 85°, hot and humid. Here in the shade of the trees, with a cool light wind rustling thru the tall grass and leaves, it must be closer to 75°. The birds are chirping. I can faintly hear Sam Vireo and his relentless song from the distance of about twenty rods (or two ponds) away. A green frog in the pond *gunks* like a broken guitar string. A mourning dove issues a plaintive cooing.

I have pulled my chair back next to the wild bee nest box, which hasn't seen much activity in the past two weeks. I'm seeking the shade at the fence line, close to the woods. I rather feel sometimes that my back is up against the wall, sitting so close as I do to the electric fence. When I removed my folding chair from the barn just now, I heard the fencer tick-tick-ticking (sending out electricity), a reminder that the fence is hot.

The breeze carries the luscious peppery scent of fresh thyme from the herb garden. A cardinal is now whistling from the ground under my menagerie of bird feeders up next to the house. Lately, all my feathered friends, the seed-eaters, that is, have been bringing their newly-fledged offspring out to introduce them to the delights of the feeders. The blue jays have been particularly fecund this year. Yesterday at our mid-day dinner (our big meal of the day here on the farm) we watched thru the sliding glass doors as Mr. and Mrs. Jay showed off their four offspring, lovely pale blue and gray birds. The youngsters hopped and squawked from the grass to the feeders to the wooden grape arbor where Mom and Dad supervised the feeding operation.

Mother Bluebird was a bit put out by all the noise and activity. She popped out of her house (where she is setting on her second set of eggs) and fluttered to the peach tree. From there Mother B. made the rounds of her usual bushes and fence posts as though to clearly delineate her territory for the jays. The blue jays paid her no mind, of course.

The antics at the feeders during dinnertime kept us all entertained. My mother-in-law, Cranberry Man, and I watched the hubbub thru the window for more than half an hour. CM regularly makes derogatory comments about the money I spend on bird food and I'm hoping someday he'll come to appreciate the value of such pleasures as birdwatching.

This is an absolutely perfect day to be alive, I think. I pause, just to enjoy being, inhaling deeply.

My heart aches, though. My childhood friend Becky passed away on Friday. "I thought I would have more time, Jenny," she said two days before she died, weeping over the telephone.

"So did I," I replied, hot tears burning my eyes. "I love you."

"I love you, too."

When I hung up, I knew that I had spoken to Becky the last in this earthly life.

The soberness of death is weighing upon me. Not anxiously or self-pityingly as one might imagine. The words of the Anglican wedding ceremony pop into my mind and, mixing it up a bit, I can hear a British-accented minister alerting his flock that they must approach death "soberly and advisedly." But no one ever does think soberly about death anymore, unless one is active in an evangelical or conservative church, and then I think death is used rather more as a scare tactic.

This is where the loss of the mainline Christian churches can really be felt in our society, for this preparation for living a good, "Godly" life by thinking soberly and advisedly about the death that is one day going to come to all of us was always their provenance. Now, many of those churches focus on social issues (necessary, but …really?). And we get our "how to" information about living and dying from those awful prescription drug commercials, from TV shows or movies, and from the internet. Many of the commercials and magazine articles encourage us to spoil ourselves in this life "because we're worth it." Or the message proclaimed is that we should live for today and other such trash. No sane person will enjoy selfishness, self-centeredness, and greed for long because when he or she follows that path they will be following it alone.

Unconditional love, healthy relationships, caring community—these require sacrifices, hard work, disinterestedness, and, most important of all, time for reflection. Time to think about what *is* important in one's life. Time to come to understand one's self and what motivates one's self—or has been motivating one's self, for it's never too late to change. Time to observe and befriend the creatures with whom we share this earth. Time to learn how to respect others—all creatures of this planet—for only then will we be able to respect ourselves. This quiet time for reflection was always to be found once or twice a week in church, and alas, for most of us, it's found no more.

It is a big responsibility to be a grown-up, and as a group we Baby Boomers have failed miserably at this duty. We have grown up to think that the world revolves around us, rather than the truth, which is that we are an infinitesimal part of an ever-revolving and evolving universe.

But it's never too late to grow up. Death will come knocking at the door of everything and everyone we love in this world. We must be prepared to answer the door courageously and gracefully so that those who come after us might take pause, take comfort, learn from our actions how to be mature, responsible adults.

Thanks to climate change we might not have much time left. I would like to see our species right itself before we exit the stage so that God might discern that we are not a complete failure.

This morning, I tedded the hay in the big hayfield belonging to one of our neighbors. The hay got rained on once and so now will be tough, but we will bring it in anyway. We have had such a struggle this year to get the first-cut hay done thanks to a superfluity of rain showers. Last year the drought; this year the rain. I don't remember such a struggle to hay 40 years ago and wonder if this, too, is related to climate change.

I finished my novel, finally, the book I started nearly two years ago, which was stalled by my mother's illness and death this winter and spring. It is such a relief to get the book done. I like the novel so much more than I thought I would when I was bogged down with the writing of it in January. But I find I'm ready to move on, ready to tackle other literary challenges.

Perhaps this change of outlook is natural, given the circumstances of this year of death. Perhaps also it is because I have allowed myself the luxury of the time—and space—for reflection. I certainly didn't think I'd head in such a sober direction when I began this nature journal in May; however, my pen has wandered where this little world under the apple tree, the scent of bee balm, sage and thyme, and where my thoughts have led me. I hope it will one day present itself as a unified whole.

I pause to listen to the cheerful birdsong. A sportscar sputters by on Route 9. The world goes on—and I feel grateful to still be a part of it.

I think Sam Vireo has gone forth and multiplied for I hear echoes of his garbled, four- or five-note song everywhere. One red-eyed vireo, in fact, has just now taken up residence in this little piece of woods and another up closer toward the house on the pond side. So much for the quiet mornings, I think, mornings like this morning, when I dozed recklessly in bed with the windows open until 7 a.m. Clearly, life goes on!

July 19, 2017

The Next Stage of Life (After Death)

Earlier this morning when I was hauling the rake behind my John Deere tractor along the South Mitchell Road (a gravel road that runs along the back side of my husband's property) what looked like one of Mr. Chippy's young offspring darted madly across the road in front of me. Sadly, it appears that neither of Mr. Chippy's children are inclined to take over their father's territory by the apple tree. Perhaps their mother (whom I rarely see or hear) wants the freedom to lure in a new mate.

It is very quiet under the apple tree without Mr. Chippy. How I miss him! I glance up from my scribbling from time to time to search the little woods, fondly regarding all the piles of dead leaves and the moss-covered rocks upon which he liked to play King of the Hill.

I'm sitting directly beneath the wild bee nest box this early afternoon. There has been no activity in the Apoidea for a long time. By my calculations, three different types of mason bees—

from very small to medium-sized—have laid eggs in the bee condominium.

Wait! As I pause to count the number of tubes mudded over, I see that the very first tube, the one mudded by our mystery bee back on June 4th has a small hole in the end of it. I rise and examine the nest box closely. Yes! The hole goes in as far as I can see (at least ½") so it's not accidental. What was in there has likely been released, though whether by its mother or by itself I do not know. I have fallen down on my bee studies lately, busy with haying and completing my novel.

Mr. Blue Jay (or one of his offspring) has started screeching. I hear Cranberry Man lumbering up the hill in his pickup, pulling a trailer full of round hay bales to put in the barn.

The air is hot and humid. I don't know how CM stands it. The hay barn is dusty and full of bird activity as the flycatchers, as well as the barn swallows, have their nests there. When I drove my tractor down thru the field earlier today (to get to the field on the other side of the South Mitchell Road), two parent phoebes led my way, flitting ahead of me from fence post to fence post, trying to distract me from their young in the hay barn. I did not have the heart to inform them that I was going that way anyway, and that I just happened to pass by their nests in the barn.

My sweat feels like a second skin. I'm hot just sitting here writing. My honeybees are moving in and out lazily—the beehive is still in the sun. I should probably get up and open the top a bit, venting the hive, but I know the hive will be in the shade shortly.

Now, compelled by guilt, I decide to go see if CM needs me to drive the truck and trailer when he goes back for the next few loads of hay.

Later, in mid-afternoon

I just picked and ate half a cupful of raspberries from my bushes before reclaiming my chair from three hours ago. The berries are amazingly sweet this year; however, there aren't many of them.

There is a noise in the leaves behind me! I peer around—I can't see from this angle. I must turn my chair.

The noise seems unlikely to be a chipmunk, for he or she would be squeaking mightily by now. Nor can the noise be caused by those prodigiously annoying jays. If I sit here quietly, occasionally stealing a glance into the woods, I will eventually figure the source of the noise. Most likely it's a small bird ground-hopping, searching for bugs.

I am going to put my feet up and just rest a bit, trying to get my being back out of the "real" world I have just left, the hustle and bustle of Waterville. I need to get back into "under the apple tree" mode, where instead of being disconnected from Mother Earth I feel as though I might be a part of it. Sometimes, however, it takes my mind a while to find its way back, like seeing a different image on a Rorschach test.

I close my eyes and listen to the various bird tweets, pinpointing the location of each feathered friend in my orbit. The chickadees. Fluttering goldfinches. Mournful doves. I feel myself relax. Inhale deeply. A moist southwest breeze caresses me, carrying on its back the sweet scent of honey from the beehive.

The apple tree branches and those tree branches above me are suddenly alive with the flutter of wings and the soft squeaks and half-calls of chickadees. Are they teaching their young to talk?

I open my eyes and scour the branches. Yes, we are having some sort of a lesson today. There is a great chickadee conversation going on from here down to the pond. I have counted at least five different voices in the mix. The calls are softer than the chickadee's mating song, so the conversation is not about sex. Good to know the birds have something else to talk about, for it sure doesn't seem as though frogs do.

I never realized until sitting here as regularly as I do how much life goes on in the world. I've been focused so much this year on the dying aspect, I think I'd forgotten that dying is a natural part of the life cycle.

Sometimes it seems strange when someone dies—like my mother, for example—and I see the world go on about its business as though nothing has changed. And nothing really has changed. What is strange is that we've come to believe the "going on" is strange. Why would we expect things to change? We should rather hope they don't, for to change from the normal cycle of Life would certainly mean death to us all.

I've become much more amiable-feeling toward death of late. I'm certainly happier to be alive, becoming more aware, more awakened, to the joy and beauty and preciousness of every moment. We go thru many changes in our attitudes toward death as we grow and mature.

At first, when we are young, we are terribly selfish and self-centered about death. It's always about us. "Woe is me! How will I live without so-and-so?" Later, when we learn to love someone other than ourselves, when we begin to develop the first tendrils of unconditional love, we feel deep grief and loss. But … this is still about our *selves*—our loss, our experience with feelings of powerlessness in relation to the beloved's suffering, which can be acute if the beloved has suffered grievously. We are loath to leave the side of their corpses even though their spirits or souls have departed and are at peace, because we have become so attached to their physical presence, the representation to us of *them*, that we still can't see that such attachment reveals to us it's still—all about us.

Where I am now physically and spiritually, I think, is a step beyond that attachment. My mind has already leapt ahead in excitement to think that my loved one—in this particular case my childhood friend, Becky—now knows the secret of the next stage of Life, for I'm sure that there is something more our souls will experience. It seems only fitting that Becky knows *first* since she was always the leader in our little group of girlfriends. She was the first to wear a garter belt, the first to get her period, the first to have sex, etc. etc.

A flycatcher takes a short hop up from the ground below the beehive and lands on the low wire of the electric fence, its brown tail bobbing up and down. I look down to write and when I glance back up, the phoebe has disappeared. But in a few seconds, I hear her landing gear go down in the dry leaves in the woods behind me. Silence. And then several rustling hops, as Phoebe searches for bugs.

Thinking of Becky's soul—her very large and wonderful spirit—having gone beyond makes me happy and at the same times almost savagely joyful of my life. When she was dying, in those last few difficult days (when she so wanted to be relieved of her suffering) there was a moment when I wanted to get in my car and race over to be by her side. But then my friend's words came back to me, giving me calm and even contentment: "I want you to remember me as I was," she said, and I knew I could give her that because, truly, dying is about the one who is passing on. To honor their wishes and carry them out is paramount. It is and should be all about *them*, not me.

When the passing has occurred, the focus naturally shifts to those left behind. And here we can offer physical support and unconditional love. But the most comfort that can be offered is to live our own lives everyday with the full understanding that death is a natural part of life and does not end the cycle, but rather is part of the continuum. This offers assurance to those left behind that there is, in fact, *more*.

Everyone by now has heard of and/or read Elizabeth Kubler Ross' stages of grieving. But we must learn to rebalance this or at least recast these stages within the stages of human growth thru which we pass in our greater understanding and experience of death, from the "Woe is me!" to the "I wonder what Becky is experiencing now?" There must be a thrill about death—not so much that one wants to seek it—but a natural wonderment about this mystery in order that we arise to greet it when death comes for us or for someone we love, joyful in spirit, perfect in contentment, assured, as Becky was, that there is *more*. The way Becky confidently marched into death like she marched into the girls' bathroom to show off her garter belt has given me an altogether more encompassing view of death. And I am grateful for Becky's confidence and courage, even as I have been grateful to have known her in the flesh.

This is the first while in many, many days when I feel the thrill of living again. Hope courses thru my veins. I am alive, and damn glad of it!

CM and I harvested four quarts of sour cherries from my two little trees. The rest I have left to three greedy ravens, who are cleaning out the branches very thoroughly, working from the top of the tree to the bottom. I baked one fabulous sour cherry pie and had the mother-in-law up for dinner, and the other three quarts I made into pie fillings and froze them for winter eating. What a treat they will be in the middle of January and February and even March! Such a small thing to bring so much joy into our lives. Cranberry Man and I will remember picking the berries together in the cool of a summer's evening.

The clouds are moving in now. The air is cooling down somewhat. A drier breeze has picked up. I think it's time for me to go ted hay on those fields of ours over on Bagley Hill. To the tractor I go!

My gladiolas and sour cherry pie.

July 29, 2017

Part of the One

We are at the height of summer now and yet I am cold. I'm sitting here under the apple tree with my legs stretched out into the sun and half-covered with a soft, light quilt. It's 75° and sunny with high clouds piling up on top of each other like waves on a beach that fail to recede. The breeze is quite brisk and from the north today, so it has icy fingers from the cold Canada jet stream.

Six of the tubes in the wild bee nest box now have holes chewed thru them, so at least six new bees have been hatched into the world. (I learned from reading my bee books that new-bees chew their way out.) There might be a whole lot more than six, however, because mason bees often lay many eggs in one hollowed-out tube. I'm going to take one of the tubes apart later in the season to inspect it, looking to see how many mini-pods or sections were created by the queen. I'm afraid to do it now because I don't want to unwittingly interrupt some slow-developing (or last laid) bee. I also read in my bee books about one species of mason bee whose queen lays the male eggs at the back of the hollow because males take the longest to hatch. Another species lays the males up front, because they are the most expendable (and thus can be placed in the situation of highest risk).

I've not written in this journal for ten days, having been out straight attempting to finish our first-cut hay, which we did (and got the hay in the barn). I was also busy polishing the first draft of my new novel, which I've now sent off to my editorial team. Phew! Now, it is time to take a bit of a well-earned break and enjoy the sights, sounds, and scents of summer.

The grasshoppers have come online since I last sat out here. I love the sound of the grasshoppers in summer, the low-key crinkling sound that gives body to the atmosphere. The sound is so ubiquitous that by the end of the summer it becomes like white noise.

The hummingbirds are squabbling over the feeders. They have become fiercely defensively lately. Cars rush by on Route 9. The fat gray squirrels leap from limb to limb in the tall trees, shaking the branches so it sounds like rain rippling thru the leaves.

A honeybee just flew right up in my face and buzzed around my nose and right eye. I ignored it. I believe it was a drone trying to get me to move my chair back a respectful distance from the hive. (I'm a bit farther forward then I usually sit today, trying to capture some warmth from the sun.) Had that been one of the worker bees I would have been stung and taught a lesson—not to sit so close and/or not to use a big brown blanket for cover, either. I probably look like a bear parked here—a life-sized Winnie-the-Pooh—which would not be a pleasant sight to a honeybee.

This morning, I made lemon lavender muffins with dried lavender buds. ("Tastes like soap," CM remarked, always very honest.) I also picked, shelled, and froze peas.

Around 11 a.m. the mother-in-law and I attended the funeral of a long-time Troy resident and local benefactress, who passed away in January at the age of 96. It was a lovely memorial service, with testimonials given by her children and grandchildren, and roses placed by her great-grandchildren. The packed service was held at the Troy Union Church, of which Grace (the deceased) had been a member and to which she donated a significant amount of money for restoration of the 1840s building.

Sitting in the pew I idly wondered (as I suppose we all do) about my own funeral, who might and might not attend. Not having children or grandchildren might lessen my chances to draw a great crowd, but then to have them is no guarantee of an abundant attendance, either. Love isn't granted simply by bearing offspring. Love comes from offering one's heart in true empathy, which is something my mother did so well and so naturally and which obviously Grace did, too. (My mother packed the church for her funeral service, which occurred during a late snowstorm in April.) I hope this gift—this desire to help others—doesn't end with my mother's and Grace's generation. It's hard for us Baby Boomers to turn our eyes around from looking at ourselves with great wonder, interest, and excitement and look rather at the world outside ourselves, out *there*. Even as I write this, I know what an impossible task this would be, for I myself have created my own little world here where I am the queen sitting on my throne, observing the comings and goings of all my subjects.

What I need to learn is not to be Lord of All (for there is only one of those), but rather to be one of the One, part of the One, who holds us all in Her hand. I am no more and no less (well, maybe somewhat less) than my hive of honeybees lazily going about their business today or the fat blue jay who squawks half-heartedly from the top of the pine tree.

A hawk of some sort circles on the breeze overhead. A crow caws three times.

I do feel different. I feel superior. Perhaps not to the hawk or the crow, or even the honeybees, but to my own kind. I feel as though I am smarter than most humans, more knowing (about what I'm sure I don't know), more self-aware (although if I could truly see how black my unconscious thoughts are most of the time, I'd be shocked).

In turning my eyes around I was going to take a good look at the world. Instead, I took a good look at my self (see how self-centered I am) and don't like what I see. I'm not a very nice person.

How many times do I avoid people seeking help when I see them coming up the driveway? I don't even like the person I see sitting in the chair. Why would I go to *her* funeral? What has she done, truly, to help others? Who does she love besides herself? Ouch, ouch.

Certainly, this is a downer of a dialogue today. Even wanting to be a better person has its roots in self-glorification, I see.

Well, I must just try to be a little bit more self-aware so that at least I know what it is I am truly observing—my self or the world. I feel the weight of sadness knowing that if few attend my funeral it will be because I have learned nothing from this day.

July 30, 2017

A Bluejay Reading Over My Shoulder

Another glorious summer day! 75° with just a few scattered clouds. Almost no breeze at all. The pond near where I am is so still, I can hear every twitter of a bird for fifty yards.

This morning, I picked basil and made pesto for our mid-day dinner and froze some pesto for winter delights. I also picked and froze some tasty chard.

The hummers are squabbling over my two hummingbird feeders, which I must refill every day, particularly the feeder that is attached to the back of the kitchen window. Apparently, the hummers like to watch me as much as I enjoy watching them! Even CM has become interested, standing and watching the tiny birds for minutes at a time, relieved temporarily from all earthly cares by the power of these creatures to suspend time by capturing our attention.

My niece Emily has asked me to read a piece on Love for her wedding this fall. I have sifted thru dozens of books (and The

Book) searching for prose pieces. Having found nothing satisfactory, I retired under the apple tree today with William Cowper, Emily Dickinson, and May Sarton, a sampling from the 18th, 19th, and 20th centuries. I can't think of a better way to be employed than to peruse the writings of these three poets while listening to my birds cooing and calling, and the bees drone, while inhaling the musky scent of bee balm emanating from my herb garden.

I gaze at that little garden, catching a glimpse of my vegetable garden beyond, framed by apple branches. The big garden is alive with startling blooms of yellow and orange calendula that popped up between the rows of vegetables as volunteers. In the background I see the garden shed with its gigantic tractor chains (for winter) hanging down the side and a mass of mustard-colored yarrow in a garden in front nearly in full bloom.

Two blue jays screech from either side of the woods. I wish they would find something else to talk about. I hear the green frogs, *gunk* more frequently than usual today. Sounds almost as though the frogs are chewing on something, noisily devouring their early supper.

The outermost berries on the tips of the blackberry canes are beginning to ripen, turning from rosy-red to dark, rich purple. Soon, we will be awash in large sweet berries. I long for my first blackberry pie of the season. This has been a good year for pies. To date I have made five or six strawberry-rhubarb pies, one sour cherry, at least two raspberry pies, and probably others I am forgetting.

Pie is my favorite food in the world. I recollect learning how to make a pie crust, how I worked and worked and worked at the dough until it was *just right.* Now, I am fine, if I don't think about what I'm doing. When I mix the flour and lard together and add ice water, I simply turn my left hand loose to work its magic, and, voila! Perfect pie crusts every time. (I'm right-handed, so when I try to mix the crust with my right hand, I overthink it.)

There is an unusual amount of road traffic for a Sunday afternoon. Perhaps people are out for a drive, since the price of gas is now so cheap. I remember not too many years ago when gas was so dear not many Mainers could afford to take a Sunday drive. One afternoon CM and I were the only ones on the road. Perhaps folks are returning from a weekend (or week) at camp? I know I would have difficulty pulling myself away from a pretty Maine lake! It's hard enough to leave the apple tree, my summer porch and favorite retreat. I'm just glad my little spot is so close to the house so that I can steal away for an hour or two's repose.

And now to the poetry I go. I hope reading these three great poets won't make me wish I was a better writer, but how could it be otherwise?

An hour later

While I was reading Cowper (pronounced "Cooper," I discovered years ago whilst watching a Jane Austen film) a blue jay alighted on a low-hanging branch and read over my shoulder. The Corvid must have liked what he read for he stayed there for several minutes, giving me the joy of reading a lyrical duet!

July 31, 2017

Postcard from May Sarton

Today is a sweltering summer day, hotter and more humid than yesterday or the day before. It's 86° or 87° in the full sun. Fortunately, my hive of honeybees and I are now in full shade, where it's eight or ten degrees cooler.

Today once again I am combing books of poetry, searching for just the right reading for my niece Emily's wedding in September. William Cowper is now out, although I so enjoyed spending some of the late afternoon with him yesterday. Cowper, talented and erudite, gives one a full course meal to digest in each poem or piece of prose. My poor brain had to work hard to keep up with the poet occasionally. I found myself re-reading stanzas several times over until I was secure in their meaning. Intrigued by Cowper's writing, I was able to wander far afield. Today I am moving on to May Sarton and Emily Dickinson, both strange and wonderful creatures and great poets in their own right.

We now need rain desperately. I water my potted plants two or three times a day. My newly-planted bleeding heart has turned yellow. The herbs in my little herb garden look dusty and wilted during the day, much like poor 19th century spinsters who can't afford to wash their clothes. My vegetable garden cries out for water, the fledgling string beans no fatter than a fork tine and have been that size for nearly a week despite the heat. Lugging the hose over to my garden is such heavy work that I naturally wait to see if Mother Nature won't oblige me and do the watering. So far, no luck.

The shallow-rooted grass in the lawn has turned yellow-brown and is brittle to the step. Only the bedstraw—that awful weed—is doing well, its roots going deep enough to pull moisture from the ground. The green patches of mown bedstraw stand out on the brown lawn like places where a man has peed.

The birds must be taking a midday siesta for there are relaxingly few tweets and chirps. A fat drone just zoomed over. He circles me briefly and zips back to the hive, apparently satisfied that I mean no harm. Or perhaps he recognized me. I always get the feeling when I'm around them that bees must be near-sighted, for they seem to have to fly up close to my face to see who it is under the apple tree. As though anyone other than me would sit so close to their busy beehive!

Behind me I hear a loud plunk and a splash. One of our Scottish Highlands has just gone into the pond to cool off. The cows like to stand in the mud, water up to their bellies. This hot weather is hard on the long-haired beasts, who although shed their heavy fur coat in spring still always walk around with the equivalent of a cashmere sweater on. The animal snorts. Water must have gotten up the cow's nose whilst drinking.

A gray squirrel has just jumped down from one of my feeders. He's making a strange vocal noise as though something might have gotten stuck in his wind pipe. (Do squirrels have both an air pipe and a food pipe, I wonder?) Now, he leaps back up on top of the feeder and curls his tail around it, hanging down to help himself to the seed below and looking like a Christmas tree ornament.

Some bird is cheeping loudly in aggravation. I can't see the bird, but the cheeps are coming from our blueberry bushes, which are near our blackberry and raspberry bushes. I suspect Robin Adair (who loves the blueberries) might have some competition for the ripe berries. Cranberry Man and I will not get many this year. I keep checking, but never beat the birds. "Why aren't the blueberries ripe yet?" CM asked me the other day. I shrugged and replied: "They are ripe. You just have to get up early in the morning to get them." "But I already get up at 4:30!" he replied. I shrugged again. "Maybe next year."

Some of the blackberries have ripened just since yesterday. If this heat keeps up, they will be ready by the end of the week. Blackberries are a fruit that even the birds don't pick before its ripe. Nobody likes a sour blackberry! I always must caution visitors who come to pick our plethora of blackberries about not nabbing the unripe berries or otherwise they would get home and bake a very sour pie or make sour blackberry jelly. It makes my mouth tingle just thinking of that tartness.

The heavy burgundy-colored blackberry canes are sagging closer and closer toward the ground, as though the burden of carrying all those berries is too much for them and they might collapse at any moment. I know I need to water them, too, but I am sweating already just sitting here and writing, I can't imagine how it would be lugging the heavy hose over and setting everything up to water the blackberries.

I glance at the sky. No sign of rain, although the app on my phone says we have a 20% chance of a thunderstorm at five o'clock. If we had hay down in the field, we would get that storm for sure!

I pause to mop some of the sweat from my face and neck. Too hot! Too hot to write, much less think. A good day to laze here doing nothing, except read poetry. This time I will not even attempt to make sense of the poems, for that is the gift of these two poets (Emily and May), who seek to touch our hearts, not our heads.

A swallow wheels in the sky above. Mother Bluebird flutters from the blackberry cane that serves as her front porch to the top of the peach tree. She unleashes a steady, excited chirping, sounding not unlike one of my teachers in high school. How I wish I understood what Mother B is saying! But even as I finish jotting these words down it has come to me like a poem that what Mother Bluebird is so cheerfully affirming is: "Life is good."

The cow in the pond snorts again. The bees circle lazily. The breeze picks up and lifts the corner of the notebook page, trying to flip the page over, letting me know beyond a shadow of a doubt that it's time to bring this entry to a close.

10 minutes later

I picked up May Sarton's little book, *A Private Mythology*, and when I opened the volume a postcard from Miss Sarton addressed to my mother dropped out onto my lap. What an amazing gift! I didn't even remember I had taken this particular book of poems from my mother's house after her death; I have been buying so many of Miss Sarton's books online lately to read. The postcard, which on the front is a photo of May Sarton's home in Nelson, NH, was written in response to a letter my mother had penned the poet. Apparently, Mom had written to tell Miss Sarton how much she liked her poetry and included a Boston Globe newspaper clipping that was a review of Sarton's new book.

It is as though my mother reached out beyond the grave to touch me today, caressing my shoulder like the soft breeze and affirming with Mother Bluebird: "Life is good!" The postcard from Miss Sarton reads:

Dear Mrs. Wixson ~ How kind of you to send me the Globe review—I had not seen it.

I am happy, <u>especially</u>, that you liked the NH poems—and that your sister-in-law felt the Japanese ones were authentic—I have had huge fan mail on <u>Pl. Dr. Deep</u> (it still goes on although the book has been out for a year), but the poems are what really matter to me.*

Bless you and thank you.

<u>May Sarton</u>

Well, I say: Bless you and thank you, May Sarton for giving me (and no doubt my mother) such a special gift!

*"Pl. Dr. Deep" is Sarton's shorthand for *Plant Dreaming Deep* (one of May Sarton's best-loved journals).

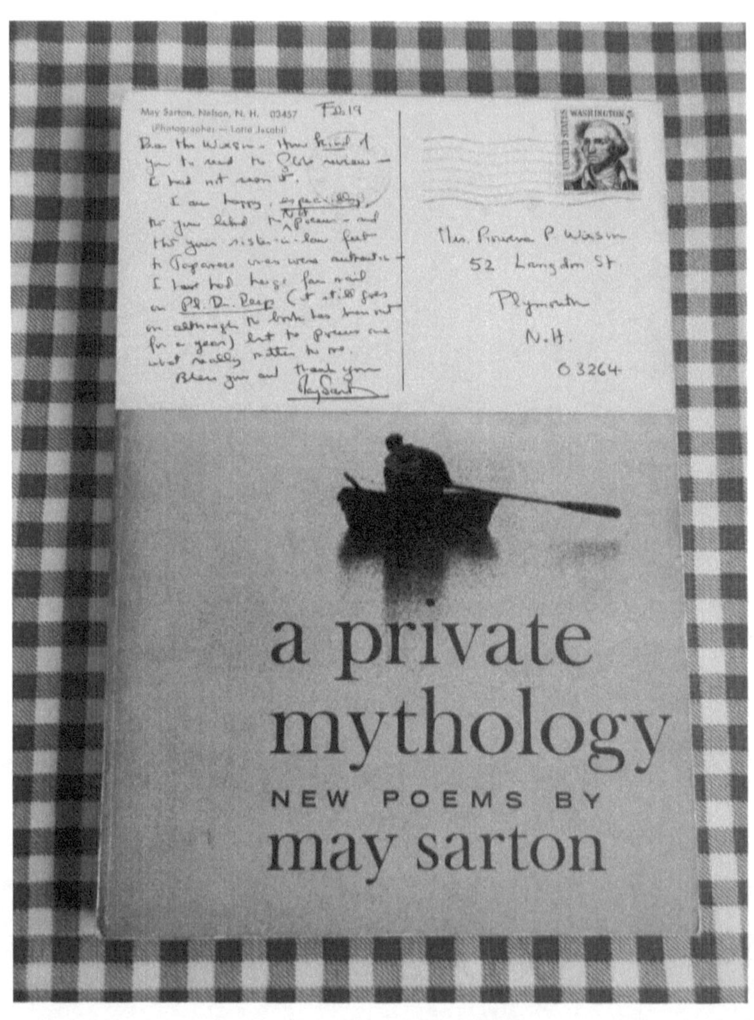

Postcard to my mother from May Sarton atop Sarton's 1966 book of poetry.

August 1, 2017

Grackles in the Ripe Blackberries

I just chased half a dozen wandering grackles out of my blackberries. I don't know why it is, but black birds seem to love black berries. The blackberries call the birds in from all over the neighborhood. Now the invading grackles are holed up in a maple tree in the woods behind me, protesting loudly. There! They have just flown off to the other side of the pond.

The blackberries are ripe. I didn't need the birds to tell me that. This morning while I was out watering my gardens, I sampled some of the lush, sweet berries. Yum! I'm going to give the berries another day or so and then set to picking in earnest, that is, if the birds leave me any to pick.

The grackles have now split up into three teams of two and have flown to the tallest trees situated in a hundred-foot radius of our house where they can watch my every move. They are triple teaming me. As soon as I leave my perch here beneath the apple tree (and I don't plan on going anywhere soon) I know they will swarm back.

Grackles are clever. They can hide quietly in the middle of the blackberry bushes, nipping the fruits down under cover where they can't be seen.

Arrgh! Two birds slipped back in while I was writing this. I started to get up to go yell at them but discovered (before leaving the chair) that one of the birds is Robin Adair and the other is from my family of blue jays. I sink back down, barely breaking a sweat. There are enough blackberries to share with my local birds. I just don't like all the uninvited tramps from Away!

Today is a repeat of yesterday, only slightly hotter and more humid. The breeze is uninspired. Both Cranberry Man and I start our work early in the morning so that by the time 2 or 2:30 p.m. rolls around—and it's too hot to work—we feel satisfied that we've done our apportioned share of labor. At least until suppertime.

We did get a half-hearted thundershower last evening, with just enough rain to wet the road. I watered my gardens for about an hour last night after the sun went down and then for another hour early this morning. And yet the ground I watered is completely dry now, thanks to such a hot day. If we don't get some rain soon, I'll need to water again.

A crow is cawing nearby, loud enough to make me conscious of his presence. He's over near CM's garden, probably picking away at something he shouldn't be.

This is the summer of May Sarton for me. Since discovering among my mother's books *Plant Dreaming Deep*, I've read more than a dozen of Sarton's journals, novels, and booklets of poetry. In fact, this journal has been inspired by Sarton's journal *Plant Dr. Deep*. I'm so happy I began this project in May and have kept at it thru the summer. My scribbling has revealed how important repose is for me, to have a regular place to go and think—or just be. A place where I am not driven hither and thither by the crazy-making news of the day; a place where I can commune with Mother Nature (and with the Divine) and with all of her subjects, my friends (and late friend, Mr. Chippy), including Robin Adair, Mother Bluebird, the native pollinators, my hive of honeybees, the jays and their family, and even the pesky grackles, who are now screeching from their ever-changing positions in the trees, watching and waiting until the vanguard (me) retires and leaves the coast clear.

The blue jay in my blackberries is calling out something. Not a warning, though. Why do I think he is telling me that the grackles are held at bay—and thus the coast is clear—if I want to come pick some berries myself?

August 5, 2017

A Storm Is Brewing

I don't know how long I'll be able to sit under the apple tree today. The wind is so strong it blew off my baseball cap while I was setting up my chair and it keeps slapping small, low-hanging branches in my face. A storm is brewing, which God knows we need. We still have not had rain. I watered all my gardens—vegetable, herb, and flower—several times.

The lady's mantle and bleeding heart have come back from the brink of death, but I'm afraid no amount of water now will save our peas. The vines are yellowing at an alarming rate, even with underdeveloped pods on them, shriveling up and dying before the peas reach full fruition.

This morning, I picked and shelled what peas both Cranberry Man and I had in our separate gardens and only ended up with a large quart to freeze. I also picked a quart of blackberries and baked a pie, but it was nowhere near as good as usual. The blackberries aren't plumping up.

There! My ballcap has blown off again. That gust of wind must have been 30mph at least. I glance over at the beehive to make sure

I have plenty of heavy rocks on top so the cover won't blow off. (I have.)

Not sure if I noted in this journal or not as the summer days are bleeding into each other so hot and dry and alike, but I captured a second swarm of honeybees in a hive I had set up for that purpose on our land on Bagley Hill. CM went up to the back of the hayfield to check on something (grass regrowth? big buck?) and he noticed the bees had taken up residence and were busy cleaning out the hive. I've been so busy myself I haven't made it over to check on the newcomers. Obviously, there are a lot more people keeping bees in this area than I'd thought, including some who don't know how to prevent their bees from swarming. (Although, in their defense, I know that once bees take it into their collective head to swarm there is almost nothing you can do to change their mind.)

Today the sky is overcast and it's around 82° with 60% humidity. I made the mistake of listening to the weatherman (and believing him that it would be cooler today) so I kept the windows open this morning allowing the fresh air to come in. By the time I finished baking the pie and blanching the peas, the house was 76° and very humid. As soon as I could (after CM went back to work from the big mid-day meal and the mother-in-law had departed) I collected my pillows and books and fled to the relative comfort of my outdoor living room.

Today I have with me a biography of sorts, *May Sarton Among the Usual Days—A Portrait.* It's a collection of her unpublished poems, letters, journals, etc. After going thru all my mother's books by Miss Sarton, I've gobbled up all her journals and novels I can find in secondhand book shops and from online used booksellers. I love her journals, in which she powerfully describes nature and the natural world, especially light or light on flowers, which blooms she planted and tended herself.

Perhaps I'm reading her letters and unpublished work now so that I will have a better understanding of May Sarton's creative forces at work. I know myself I write best and produce the most when I'm grounded and tied to the land, such as here in Troy or at my former home in Winslow (my great-grandparent's place,

Sunshine Cottage), where I lived and wrote happily for a decade during my younger years. I know that it is a good day when I pick and can string beans, feed and kiss my husband, water my plants, feed my birds (a blue jay is screeching now, squabbling with a family of crows over the blackberries, no doubt), and pick up a pen.

I fear that my friend Sam Vireo has already departed for warmer climes, winging his way back to South America. I have not heard his loud, unflagging melody either in the morning or at any other time of day. Perhaps a week or so ago, when I heard many vireo voices around the pond, Sam's friends were stopping by from Away to gather him and his family up to add to their troupe for the long journey south. It seems early to me for the vireos to leave, and although I'm sad to see Sam go, I'm already looking forward to next spring—to the first day he returns to our little pond. Already I am tasting some of that joy in contemplating that day.

Now, to Miss Sarton I go, for my notebook page is full. I am running out of space to write, and not willing to turn the page today.

Me shelling peas on our front porch.

August 6, 2017

The Heatwave Breaks

Our hot dry spell broke last night with a welcome thunderstorm that dumped ¾-inch of rain in less than an hour. Today the weather is 72° and sunny with some poufy white clouds scudding about. The air is refreshing, having been cleansed and purified by the storm.

Likewise, my soul is undergoing a similar purification. I awoke this morning around 4:30 a.m. in a state of Dread. I have sensed the paralyzing fear approaching, dreading even the advent of Dread. I lay in bed tensed and tingling with flashes of hot and cold, unable to move, so small and mean and worthless did I feel. I could not even seek solace from Cranberry Man as I literally could not move a muscle. The Dread engulfed me. I felt as though my veins were filled with sawdust, my muscles, old rags—useless, oil-soaked, dirty old rags.

This all-engulfing feeling of Dread has come upon me once before. It happened when I was in seminary, after I officiated at a funeral for a 12-year-old girl who was killed by a hit-and-run drunk driver. That Dread, which lasted for several days, eventually led me to a deeper insight into the human condition. It became an opportunity to see how selfish and shallow I really was, a nasty but necessary viewing, sort of like seeing myself at my own wake and hearing as Scrooge did what people really think of me. My scalp tingles with mortification as I recollect that awful vision.

When we are in this state of Dread—keenly aware of the absolute hopelessness of our spiritual condition—we are finally able to see that there is no hope but to turn to God. Even when we turn to the Divine, however, we do not experience relief. No. Rather the opposite. We must employ our faith. We must grit our teeth, get up out of bed, clothe ourselves, and go back to work, putting one leaden foot in front of the other. We must force ourselves to go on in the blackness, the emptiness, the abyss, having faith that the One Who Calls Us Into Being is willing this experience for our own good, although this is impossible to believe at the time. Indeed, I do not believe this now as I write these words, rather I feel terror in my bones. My hands shake. My teeth are clenched. But … forward I go, for there is no going back and standing still is so horrible it is certainly not an option.

So, this morning I went over to our project house (an old post-and-beam restoration project where CM spends much of his time) and I put up two walls of faced-batt insulation, a task I have been dreading, but not as much as I have the approaching spiritual Dread. I might as well work thru two dreads at the same time, I reasoned. How bad could the insulation project be—the cutting and stuffing and stapling of those pink cotton-candy batts that cling to you, scratching your skin, eyes, and nose—when one feels one's soul is worthless?!

After lunch I cleaned the kitchen. I remember my mother cleaning—always cleaning! —when she was under duress. As though one could whitewash a soul by cleaning the home in which one's physical body resides or even by cleaning the body itself!

I know the Dread is related to my mother's death. I keep running several scenes—the same ones—thru my head. I won't make it worse by describing them here; it's bad enough that the scenes keep playing over and over, cutting me sharply, as though God is using the images as a tool to whittle me into humility. (It's working.) It seems like a paradox, but I think one must be truly humbled to be emancipated from one's rapacious self.

A really interesting bee—some sort of thin, scrawny sweat bee—has landed on my lap pillow. He has a very long black antenna or tongue that is vibrating valiantly, trying to suck nectar from the faux brown leather. Discouraged because there is nothing there, he lifts his tongue and flies away. What strange creatures populate this planet! Every day I discover new ones.

There are still about a dozen bees or pods left to hatch in my wild bee nest box. I noted today as I set up my chair that the first of the white fabric-looking filled tubes has a hole chewed thru the end. I wish I could stumble upon a new bee chewing its way out! How fun and interesting that would be. I know three different bees utilized my nest box this summer, but my studies haven't yet led me to figure out which ones those might be. The more time I spend with my honeybees (and today they are seriously working, perhaps a dozen or so coming in with nectar as the same number are going out) the more I learn about them and the more filled with peace I feel. I find the activity—the sights, sounds, and smells—of honeybees a very calming experience. Now the goldenrod is in bloom; however, I don't think they've been putting up much goldenrod honey because when they do the hive emits the odor of dirty socks and I haven't smelled that yet. (The goldenrod honey tastes fabulous, though.)

My teeth are no longer gritted. My right leg is relaxed. I can hear the crickets and grasshoppers singing, which I couldn't when I first arrived because my focus was on myself and was so dark I could barely stumble over the ground to get here. I gaze around and note with pleasure the grass has greened up some overnight. We badly need the rain. There are still some brown patches where the bedrock is close to the surface, but now the green is more extensive than the brown.

A worker bee just came over to inspect me. I can tell the difference between a worker bee and a drone by their sounds. A drone is much louder and buzzes more angrily than a worker, but drones can't sting so I usually ignore them. The worker bees, however, could decide I am a threat to the hive—take offense at my nearness—and sting me. Or if I have the temerity to look at them when they fly over to me (which I don't, I'm always very careful to pull back into myself and humbly avert my eyes), they will zip up to my head or eyes and find some soft place to impale their stinger. This agitated bee, after buzzing slowly in and out around me, has apparently deemed me harmless and returned to the hive.

I think this pulling in of my Self is just what is needed now. Altogether I am too much *out there*, filled with too much self-confidence, too much "in your face" all the time. Just thinking of how I am sometimes makes me shudder.

A lime-green caterpillar with black legs, a black head, and black nobs down its spine, is inching along the right arm of my chair. I marvel at the perfect symmetry of coloring on the creature. Too bad Sam Vireo has departed for he could have enjoyed an afternoon snack. I flick the caterpillar onto the ground with my pen (which takes three or four attempts, for the insect clings to the arm as though it was something good). Now he lies unmoving on the ground, head resting on a brown, dead leaf, as if the fall was too much for him. Perhaps the terror of the free-fall killed him. I will keep an eye on him. (Long pause.) No movement yet. I flick a couple of small sticks at him. There is the slightest of pullbacks, but really the poor thing just looks shell-shocked. The ants will soon have their way with Mr. Green Jeans if he's not careful!

I brought with me my favorite summertime novel to read, *Country of the Pointed Firs* by Sarah Orne Jewett. Every summer I treat myself to a visit to Dunnett's Landing in Down East Maine. It's better than an actual road trip, for Jewett takes me back into the 19th century, into the cozy house with herself and Almiry Todd, the local herbalist and apothecary. I love Almiry's mother, Mrs. Blackett, who resides on Green Island with her son William (Almiry's brother). Taking the skiff out on a windy day to visit with Mrs. Blackett gives me hope that my mother, like this sweet, child-like elder, who fixes fish stew on her woodstove for lunch, still lives *out there* in some strange and wonderful universe.

The clouds have swept nearly all the blue from the sky. A carpet of gray is forming in the Heavens. Mr. Green Jeans is now climbing up one of the long twigs I tossed at him. A stairway to nowhere, as he will soon discover. But at least I know he is alive and can take comfort that I haven't needlessly killed one of God's innocent creatures today. (Although I did deliberately step on an ant in the house earlier.)

When one is under the influence of Dread, one feels at the bottom of the totem pole, rather than a keystone species. What an interesting world this would be if humans were subjects of the insect world. Perhaps we are and don't know it, for surely the ants will conquer the Earth.

I wonder if Mr. Green Jeans knows where he's going? He's now inching slowly along thru the grass in the direction of the beehive. Or is he just moving forward? Because, like me, that is what he must do?

Keep—moving—forward.

August 9, 2017

Summer Seeping Away

The sun is shining thru the clouds. The air is moist and warm, almost like bathwater. The cadence of the grasshoppers' song is very relaxing. The dozens of starlings who have done a very clean and thorough job picking my ripe blackberries are now chatting about their satisfying adventure from the crowns of the black locust trees over by the grandparent's barn. Life is good.

The Dread I experienced has passed, leaving in its wake a calmness and a feeling of well-being. There is a sweetness in the air I never noticed before the Dread, a sweet intangible smell of Life rather than a scent of the corporeal, such as my herbs. (I have been cutting rosemary, thyme, and sage for drying so my hands smell very fragrant.)

I feel more connected to something greater than myself, to the natural world and to society. My spirit floats upon the sublime and yet I'm tethered like a tied helium balloon. I wouldn't want to float completely free, afraid I'd become like some of the trash in space, wandering and floating out there forever.

I hear the crickets chirping at night now. It's impossible not to notice that summer is seeping away. The days are getting shorter.

It is no longer light out at 4 a.m. when I arise. This morning, only the faintest of rosy glows colored the eastern horizon. My friend Sam Vireo has fled, although two days ago I did hear another red-eyed vireo at our project house across town while I was putting up insulation. Today, however, even that vireo made itself scarce.

The hummingbirds are still with us, darting and buzzing and zipping about as they defend their feeders. When the hummingbirds fly south, I'll know that my time under the apple tree is over. Soon it will be time to harvest the rest of the garden—corn, squash, pumpkins, tomatoes—and the cranberries will need tending. CM says we will not have a big crop this year thanks to the drought, but he says that every year so I'll wait and see. (The last crop we harvested was 6,000 pounds.)

The starlings have returned for a second picking of blackberries. Oh, how cheerful their little squabbles sound! Such a babbling and chatting! The berries are small and seedy this year and so I've decided I don't mind sharing them with the greater avian community. Before taking up my pen, I grazed upon the blackberries myself, searching out the plump berries the starlings had missed on their first picking.

Something scares the birds off and they lift like a dark wave, nearly a hundred wings aflutter. Shadows flee at their heels, making the flock seem twice as large as it is.

My honeybees were eagerly putting up goldenrod nectar around lunchtime, but now they have settled back into their regular, steady pace. In a week or two—before the bloom of the goldenrod has entirely passed—I will remove the last box of honey and let them fill their two deeps for winter.

Last night I picked, snapped, and canned my first canner-full of string beans (both green and wax). I need to freeze more spinach. Unfortunately, the peas passed before all the pods filled out. (Doesn't that sound like a song? ~ "The peas passed before the pods popped …") As a result, I was only able to freeze two quarts of peas. Nothing is so good in the dead of winter as steamed peas from our garden with a roast chicken, baked potato, and a cherry or raspberry pie. Oh, the meals I am looking forward to already!

My herbs are currently drying on the dehydrator, filling our house with the most delightful scent. My gladiolas are in bloom and every day I pick a fresh bouquet. I feel quite rich, and yet the actual price of the bulbs in legal tender was quite small and the elbow grease only modest. My sister from Stonington stopped by today and remarked how lovely the yellow glads looked with the pompoms of blue globe thistle added to the arrangement for contrast.

The apples in the tree above me are the size of tangerines. From where I sit, I can see more than a dozen of the round green globes. Some of them fell during the summer drop season, but not all by any means. And the two ancient Duchess of Oldenburg trees in the field across the road have more apples on them than I've ever seen before. It's going to be a good apple year, which means the blossoms had good pollination in the spring. Thank you, honeybees and native pollinators!

I have begun to think about my next writing project, now that I can see the end of this one (my novel) drawing near. When I first came out of the teeth-chattering abyss of dread, I thought I'd like to create something beautiful. I even dared to allow my mind to linger on the possibility of poetry, which is very startling as I don't think I've written a poem since I was ten-years-old. John Keats' line keeps running through my head: "A thing of beauty is a joy forever." I want to create that thing of beauty, but there are days when I can scarce rub two words together the right way, let alone six or seven.

A large, fat bumblebee just moseyed over and checked out my bare leg. Not much of interest there; he flies off. The drones are returning to the hive from their mid-day marauding, looking for virgin queens. How frustrated they must be! (I know none of them scored, because drones die when they mate.) Maybe there are a lot more virgin queens around here than I think for, though. After all, I did pick up two swarms of bees this summer, so at least two drones might have got lucky (and paid the ultimate price) with the virgin queens that were hatched and remained with the old hives.

My stomach rumbles and I wonder if the starlings have missed any ripe blackberries. I will amble over to see.

The four quarts of blackberries I picked the other day.

August 10, 2017

Cheerful Crickets and Bumblebees in the Herb Garden

The bumblebees are loving my herb garden today. I pulled my chair back next to the wild bee nest box (I'm determined to see one of those new hatchlings chew its way out), placing the chair between the cedar fence post and the herb garden. More than a dozen of the fat, yellow-and-black insects swarm over my blue globe thistle and mauve-colored sedum, which is also in bloom.

The crickets are cheerful. I feel very alive today. I've been sitting out here—reading, dozing, and relaxing—for almost two hours, my reward for a hard morning insulating at our project house, where that scratchy, glassy, pink stuff gets into my eyes, nose, and skin. The sweat pouring over my face and down my neck and back only makes it worse.

Now some of the bumblebees have moved to the wild bergamot bee balm, with its lovely purple blossoms. Honeybee tongues aren't long enough to reach the nectar in the herbs this afternoon—or something else (likely the goldenrod) is calling them—for there are none in my herbs at all.

Some bird cries loudly from the other side of the pond, but it is quiet up here on the hill. Wait! I just heard the soft cooing of a mourning dove. So sad, so plaintive, yet so peaceful-sounding.

The sky is completely clouded over. The barometric pressure is dropping. (The honeybees will like that—pushes the nectar in the blooms further out.) A storm is blowing in. Strong gusts of wind toss the apple tree branches and even the great branches of the oak around as though they were boats on a stormy sea.

The air is fresh and fecund-smelling, carrying a scented touch of pond water on its back. Traffic is racing by out on Route 9, as though the drivers know something and can't wait to get to where they are going to share the news. I'm glad they pass me by. I don't need to know.

My rest is nearly over. As soon as my work pants are dry, I must weed-whack around the foundation of our project house. Cranberry Man has started to paint the clapboards on the east side, clapboards that he made from wood he cut on his own land. He is so resourceful and hardworking. I used to try and keep up with him, but no more. I prefer to work some, rest some, read some, write some … and count bumblebees. Now there are fourteen bumblebees in the herb garden! Which of us is the better employed?

Cranberry Man working at our project house, putting up his homemade clapboards.

August 14, 2017

Never Alone Under the Apple Tree

My honeybees are very busy today. The air in front of the hive is a regular traffic jam so many bees are trying to come and go at the same time. They must be on the goldenrod this lovely August afternoon.

The crickets are chirping loud and cheerful. A swallow or two flutters and cheeps from the belly of my blackberry bushes. The swallows won't get many ripe berries, though. That loot was carted off earlier by the starlings. Cranberry Man showed me where the starlings have been attacking his sweet corn, too. Several ears on the north end of his patch have been ripped into. There is no evidence of corn borers this year, however, so perhaps the birds have paid for their dinner in advance by eating the moths that lay the eggs that turn into European corn borers.

Behind me in the woods—just below the hay barn—I hear a cow snort. Sounds like a horse.

Today is dry and 80°, with a light breeze and clouds just beginning to creep in around the edges of the skyscape. The clouds wash the turquoise-blue of the sky down to a pale, slate-gray color.

The crickets are singing that fall is approaching. Already the evenings are so cool that sometimes I must get up and close the windows at night lest the house be too cold when we arise.

I'm sad that summer is almost over. In Maine, the season passes so quickly, at least here on the farm. When I was a young child, summer seemed to last forever. But then three months is a long time when one is only five or six years old. When one is sixty, three months isn't much. Time speeds up when one ages, although I suppose it's just our impression of time—how much has gone before compared to how much might be left to come. I noticed a shift in my perception of Time in my mid-thirties. Perhaps unconsciously I thought I was passing the half-way mark of my life. I hope not.

The hummingbirds are still here, though, as are the geese that fly from pond to pond, fooling me with their loud honking thinking that they might be forming to fly south. Usually on hearing the overhead alarm I dash to the window (or look up, if I'm outside) to ascertain what direction the wild geese are flying and if they are in formation. I want to hold onto summer like the reins of a runaway horse and try to muscle it to stop. Not much luck so far, nor did I ever have much luck with runaway horses!

I have been working on writing a poem for niece Emily's wedding, having discovered nothing suitable yet. Unfortunately, I've also discovered I'm a terrible poet.

Behind me, the cow snorts again. And again. I wonder if she has something (hay chaff? a bug?) up her nose. I hope it's not a moose back there in the woods. Whatever the creature is, it's a lot closer than the animal I thought was a moose when I began this journal in May. I should turn around to look, but I do not.

The flock of starlings is back. Dozens of them zip through the blackberry bushes picking off what little is left of the ripe berries. I knew I should have eaten my fill before I sat down! Now there will be no more ripe blackberries until tomorrow at the earliest. Even then, I'll have to work hard to beat the birds. But there is something endearing about the starlings' soft squawks and flutters. Their birdsong is very musical and full-bodied, as there are so many of them. I imagine each squawk an exclamation of delight, a bird "Ah! That was good." And audibly I count the number of berries being consumed by each outpouring of delight.

I don't think CM will enjoy their music very much if the birds take to his sweet corn. I told him he needs a scare balloon for his corn patch, but he shrugged it off. He doesn't realize how much of our treasure the birds have already hauled away in their bellies—almost two complete and heavily-set sour cherry trees AND most of the blackberries. By rights, each of these starlings should weigh about ten pounds and should barely be able to fly.

The flock has now flown off en masse to the black locust trees, where they like to hang out. Only yesterday did CM notice all the bird droppings on his old truck parked over there. "I guess I shouldn't have left the truck under the trees," he remarked. No, probably not. And I guess that might be a sign of, A. how many birds there are, and, B. how close they are to his corn, which is only a few yards away from his truck!

A crow caws out a warning. To whom and about whom I'm not sure. The crows and ravens have really taken a back seat to this flock of starlings, which now lifts off and is entertaining me with a dance in the sky. The black birds float over this way and then split into two even groups, one group turning west and the other turning east. The birds come around again, joining back up as one gorgeous circle. The black murmuration floats away over the hay barn.

Sometimes, I think I should feel lonelier than I do, especially with my mother gone. (Even now, I still pick up the phone to call her.) But then I look at my herb garden and notice all the bumblebees going about their business, moving meticulously through every floret on a single flower or herb, not rushing, not skipping onto the next delight until the nectar in every petal, every floret, has been exhausted. And watching the bees—both wild and my own honeybees—I don't feel the least bit lonely. How could I? I'm never alone under the apple tree. There is always some living creature—be it bird or bug or frog or chipmunk or squirrel or flower or herb or tree—to let me know I'm not alone, that the weight of the world does not rest on my shoulders. I feel part of a crowd out here, there are so many of us doing our thing and I'm just one of "them." My job is to *be* and to record what I see, hear, smell, taste, and sense in the world around me.

The air is dry today, very dusty-smelling. Not terribly fragrant. Perhaps it's the dying embers of scent from the wild bergamot bee balm and cooking herbs (thyme and sage), wilting in my herb garden. I know I should probably water everything again, but the weatherman has promised an 80% chance of rain on the morrow and I'm lazy enough to want to wait and see if Mother Nature won't do my work for me.

My cellphone rings, interrupting me. I fumble for it. No one is there. Very frustrating! Why do I even bring the damn thing out here?

To tell the time. Because I don't have a watch.

Well, the time is … time to buy a watch and leave the phone inside! This is meant to be *my* time, not time at the command of just anyone who happens to call my number. Now that Mom is deceased, there is no one who really needs to get hold of me *right now* (well, except my husband and my 88-year-old MIL). Sigh. The phone will stay, but I'll be more judicious in deciding whose calls to answer.

No wonder our time slips away! We are so at the mercy of others in this technological age. My phone makes all sorts of intriguing plinks and plings when someone replies to one of my tweets or "likes" something I post on Facebook. Those tech titans know just what sounds will prompt us to pull up our screens, wasting even more of our precious time. No, it's back to the watch idea! I can't stand the thought of those plinks and plings replacing the pleasant cadence of the crickets and grasshoppers or the hope-filled sounds of the spring peepers and tree frogs. Give me nature any day, for she is natural, especially compared to the unnatural noises of my cell, which remind me of all the bells and whistles and flashing lights on a slot machine.

There should be a law that everyone—in summer, anyway—be required to sit out under an apple tree or beside a lake or ocean without a phone or other mobile device for at least two hours a day. How that would alter our sensibilities for the good! I know I'm a better person after sitting here for an hour or two than when I first arrived. Something generally upsets my equilibrium every day, yet when I return to the house after spending time with all my nature buddies, I feel mentally whole, physically healthy, and emotionally well-rounded. Spiritually, I feel connected to something greater than myself, something infinitely superior to human consciousness, something that will continue long after I am gone. I feel my spirit spiral upward, a similar impression of "rising up" that I experienced when I healed myself from alcohol addiction. I felt this sensation also when I was at seminary; when I had my church; when I performed my first funeral service—and when I dug the hole at the cemetery to bury my mother's ashes.

There is *more*, and we are a part of it. Death is not the final chapter in Life; death is *part* of Life.

I wrote earlier in my journal that, for me, this was going to be the year of death. Now, I see how wrong I was. This is the year of Life, and my mother and Becky (and Mr. Chippy) now know the next stage of Life beyond this one. Amen to them. I will see you again!

Mom’s grave in Norway Pine Grove Cemetery.

August 23, 2017

August Is a Month for Laziness

I have not written for a while, it having come into my head that I should write more in this journal about death, thereby breaking my own rule that I write what the spirit moves after I sit down, not pre-planned. Well, here I am … and I am still dogged by death.

But I don't want to write of death as a Thing unto itself. I want to consider—and do now consider—death as a part of life. A thin veil separates us from the unknown; however, that the veil can be breached and the journey continued I have no doubt.

This is another lovely August afternoon. August is my favorite month, and not just because I was born in August. I hear the sweet, high-pitched song of the grasshoppers rubbing their back legs against their forewings. The sun shines. The breeze stirs one's soul. August is a month to enjoy just being—it's not a month to concentrate on getting things done (although my honeybees are busy putting up goldenrod today, I see!)

August is a month for trivial reflections, a time for laziness, for letting go of lists and appointments and "must dos." (For example, I feel as though I really must invite some of Cranberry Man's extended family out for dinner; however, I can't make myself pick up the phone and make an actual date.)

As I write, I hear some of my neighbor's granite being loaded onto a tractor trailer truck. More of Maine's stone walls, stoop stones, and/or grist wheels and well covers are no doubt going out of state. I always feel sad when I hear the granite being loaded, thinking of the old-timers whose labor to move and stack the stones ended in such futility. Makes me wonder at my own endeavors, how futile will be my long-time struggle as a writer? Is it even worth the effort? Like the old-timers, however, I can't *not* try to pile up "rocks," try to wrest something out of nothing, utilizing whatever Mother Nature has to offer.

I rest my left elbow on the arm of the chair and stare off to the east. Such a pretty prospect! A blue sky and branch of the apple tree frame my little herb garden. The honeybees are active on purple blooms of the wild bergamot and slate-blue horsemint blossoms. Fat bumbles flit here and there, spending most of their time on the prickly, blue globe thistle. The light breeze from the southwest springs up and carries a musky scent from the beehive to my nose. I inhale deeply, holding my breath for twenty seconds or so. Yes, the bees are putting up goldenrod honey. It is the smell of dirty socks!

In an hour or two CM and I have a date to go "shopping" through that very same neighbor's field of granite. (He buys and sells granite for his livelihood.) We are looking for a stoop stone for our project house so we'll keep at least one of those granites in Maine. I traded our neighbor twenty pounds of our grassfed, grass-finished burger for the stone, which will be used as a step to the front door of the post-and-beam house, which belonged to my late friends and neighbors Stella and Raymond Cook. (Our restoration project is a labor of love, to save an old house, but also an investment.) I don't feel badly re-purposing this old granite for it was a common practice in Maine to do so. After Stella and Ray died, the poor old place was left vacant for many years before CM and I purchased it from their daughter, who lives out of state. I wonder when I pass thru the veil of death what Stella and Ray will have to say about what we have done with their "castle," as they used to describe their home. I hope they like it.

I am plagued by small black ants, and I'm sitting in my usual spot. I peruse the ground beneath and around my chair. I don't see any abnormal insect activity—not any ants at all—so perhaps I accidentally placed my pillows upon the ant's nest when I set them down to fetch the chair from the barn. Quickly, I brush off both pillows and check my clothing. All gone. At least they weren't red ants; I hardly felt them crawling over my bare arms.

The drones are returning to the hive. It must be close to three o'clock. They make such a loud and showy buzzing noise when they come in so I know it's them without looking up. I've always found drones rather funny, especially as I know and they don't (at least, I don't think they know) that when fall arrives they will be tossed out of the hive for good. The worker bees can't afford to feed the lazy drones over the winter. Let them have their fun now. Their season will soon be past and soon the drones, too, will pass beyond the veil. NOTE TO SELF: Do not assume that drones still cannot sting when you meet them on the other side.

The other evening, I overheard a YouTube video CM was playing about a new drug that promised to reverse the aging process. It was some sort of Fountain of Youth pill that would enable one to remain in the same physical condition one is in when he or she starts taking the pills. As I listened, it came into my head that death was not a bad thing, but a good thing. I thought of the humbling I received during my days of Dread and realized how arrogant and selfish humans would become if we were to live forever, with nothing to dread. What a horrible picture! Suddenly, I wanted to leap up and defend death, of all things. Me? Defending death? How I have changed my thinking in just a few months!

The notebook paper feels smooth and comforting to my touch as I rub my fingertips against the blue-lined page. I am glad I'm here to feel the paper; to think; to be. To see the flitting shadows on the lawn of the songbirds darting overhead. To hear the joyful noise of the crickets. To see the dappled sunlight splash across my herb garden. Delicate white blooms of Queen Anne's lace—wild carrot—bob in the breeze.

It is good to be alive. I feel some satisfaction to think that I am still on this side of the veil. I still have time to love, to write books, to feed my birds and chipmunks, to water my plants, to send off little notes of encouragement and care packages to my nieces and nephews, and to shop for old granite in my neighbor's most unusual garden of stones.

My lawn chair under the apple tree next to my herb garden, with the fence and my John Deere tractor in the background.

September 4, 2017

All But One Hummingbird Has Flown

What a gorgeous afternoon! It's nearly 80° and very balmy, although milky-white clouds are pushing in with the promised and much-needed rain later this afternoon.

This will probably be my last entry in this journal and no doubt my last opportunity for rest and reflection under the apple tree this year. All but one small female hummingbird has left me. I still keep the two feeders up, though, for her and for the hummingbirds that pass through Troy on their way south.

As always at the end of the season, summer feels like it was much too short. And yet I recollect many, many afternoons and mornings when I enjoyed my repose here. Time stands still when I disappear under the outstretched arm of the apple tree with all my companions beside the little woods, up above the frog pond.

One of my favorite memories from this summer was the afternoon I startled Walter the tree frog by snapping a flash pic of him while he was singing away in his hidey-hold in the maple tree.

(Probably not Walter's favorite moment from this summer!) And where would I be without having had Mr. Chippy in my life? I loved to sit and watch him go about his business, back and forth from my bird feeders with his fat, stuffed cheeks to his winter abode under the bee hive's pallet. As I write, I hear the familiar monotonous cheeping of a chipmunk (one of Mr. Chippy's children) behind the hay barn and I feel joy knowing I will have company under the apple tree next summer. Now, the squeaking has been acknowledged and reciprocated by a chipmunk from across the pond. The circle of life goes on!

How many friends have I made this year, by taking the time to step into their little world! The hard-working Mother Bluebird; my early-rising and indefatigable friend Sam Vireo; Mr. & Mrs. Hairy Woodpecker and their flighty family; a wide variety of wild bees, natural pollinators, whose nesting habits I've studied; and so many more. In fact, my Apoidea still has mudded-off tubes. All the early bees have hatched, but the "girls" have continued to lay eggs in more than a dozen tubes, filling them with a variety of different stoppers, everything from dried yellow and tan mud, to white linen-ish looking stuff.

But ... many of the songbirds have departed, Sam Vireo being the earliest, and now the hummingbirds the latest. Golden apples covered with a red blush are beginning to fall from the tree. It's time to say goodbye. Time to move on.

We have finished our second—and last—cut of hay, which was very small due to lack of rain. Next up is harvesting the rest of the garden. Fall and its many chores—and glorious vistas of foliage—is a special season, but autumn is a time of activity, of bringing in wood and washing summer's dust and pollen off the windows. Fall is not a time to laze away beneath the apple tree.

An apple plops to the ground. It's a gift to take away with me. Goodbye, tiny world! Goodbye, my dear friends! I will look for you next spring. May our relationship continue to deepen year after year—here—under the apple tree.

An apple on my special tree.

September 26, 2017

Indian Summer (Epilogue)

We have been experiencing the most prolonged summer weather. As a result, I have sought the delights of my spot under the apple tree one last time before the chilly winds of fall—with winter hard on its heels—close the gate for good. I hear plashing in the pond and spy some of my Scottish Highland cattle, perhaps six or seven of them, cooling off in the mud and water. It's 88° in the sun and about 82° in the shade, with a light breeze.

Despite the unseasonable warmth, it is well and truly fall in central Maine. The leaves are turning brown and there is already a crisp pile of them beneath my feet. It's precarious sitting here for every now and then, at the most inopportune moment, an apple (or acorn from the burr oak) drops and thumps me in the head. Even when the missile misses it startles me. I jump a bit in the chair, for the apples and even the acorns are loud when they hit the ground.

A gorgeous orange monarch butterfly flies up to me. I hold my breath. She flutters around and lands on my floral-pattern pillow, her wings slowly opening and closing, like lungs breathing in and out. What a miracle to behold!

One of the cows (sounds like Delilah) moos softly and then offers a louder bellow, no doubt calling for her late-season calf. Her milk has probably let down. We had two very unexpected fall calves on the farm this year. Our steer Archie turned out not to be a steer at all! (One of the rubber castrating bands we put on his testicles must have broken.) Now we are back to where we started last summer when we sold our herd bull Merlin so that we could gradually reduce our herd in order to retire. Archie has since gone to claim his Great Reward, but not until he was able to breed most of our cows again. That, I think, was his main reward.

The crickets are chirping and the grasshoppers are singing. The woods smells like musty, decomposing vegetation. My honeybees are very active, bringing in nectar from my late-blooming herbs, from my basil that has gone to seed, and from the purple asters and other fall flowers. Altogether, despite the heat and humidity, it's a gorgeous day. I really feel as though we have stolen an extra day from fall to add to the scales of summer.

All the wild bees in my nest box have finally hatched. The hollow tubes are open again, clean and inviting for next year's brood. My songbirds have deserted me. Even the chickadees and blue jays, who will surface when the snow begins to fly, are getting their feed elsewhere than my feeders because there is so much available in the natural world right now. Mr. Chippy's son (or daughter) is about my only visitor to the feeders these days. But I'm so glad to make his or her acquaintance that I keep the feeders stocked fresh with black-oil sunflower seeds.

Kerplunk. Bounce, bounce goes an apple from the tree. A sodden tree limb in the woods snaps, sounding much like the first day I began this journal, when I wondered if a moose was nearby. The butterfly still rests on my pillow, wings lifting half-heartedly, but showing no real desire to depart.

An acorn falls, crashing down from limb to limb, as acorns are want to do. I hope it grows to become a big, beautiful oak tree. I like the thought of someone in the future seeking from the oak shade and solace, much as I have done under the apple tree.

I have been given a great gift this year and all I did to receive such a blessing was to bring myself here, away from the world, and be open to the goings-on in this small bit of woods near the pond. Mother Nature—God's busiest evangelist—found me this summer, and it was good.

Delilah is still mooing. I fear she has misplaced her calf again and so I must go and help her find the little tyke. Time to fly, butterfly!

Delilah's calf, separated from its mother (again).

OTHER WRITINGS BY JENNIFER WIXSON

Fiction
Hens & Chickens (Book 1 in *The Sovereign Series*)
Peas, Beans & Corn (Book 2)
The Songbird of Sovereign (Book 3)
The Minister's Daughter (Book 4)
Maggie's Dilemma (Book 5)

Non-fiction
Learning to SOAR!
A History of the Crockett Family of Crockett's Ridge, Norway Maine
"Into the Maine ..." ~ One Maine Family's Quest for Land, 1630-1830

ABOUT JENNIFER WIXSON

Maine farmer and author Jennifer Wixson writes from her home in Troy where she keeps bees and raises Scottish Highland cattle and cranberries. A graduate of the School of Hard Knocks, Jen also admits to a Master's Degree in divinity from Bangor Theological Seminary.